TUTANKHAMEN'S TREASURE

Howard Carter

Howard Carter was born in Norfolk in 1873. At the age
of 17 he made his first visit to Egypt as a draughtsman
for an archaeological survey conducted by the Egypt
Exploration Fund. After much archaeological research
and experience in Egypt he was appointed in 1899 as
Inspector General of the Antiquities Department of the
Egyptian Government, in which capacity he discovered
the tomb of Mentuhetep and began his excavations in the
Valley of the Kings. In 1908 Carter joined the fifth Earl
of Carnarvon who was carrying out a series of
archaeological investigations in Thebes. The discovery
of the tomb of Tutankhamen, on 4th November, 1922,
was the crowning achievement of Carter's brilliant career;
hardly less of an achievement was the systematic and
painstaking work of cataloguing all the objects found in
the tomb, and in their transport to the Cairo museum,
which took ten years to complete (1922–1932). Howard
Carter published the original edition of THE TOMB OF
TUTANKHAMEN in three volumes from 1923–1933.
He died in London in 1939.

TUTANKHAMEN'S TREASURE

Tutankhamen's Treasure

HOWARD CARTER

SPHERE BOOKS LTD
30/32 Gray's Inn Road, London, WC1X 8JL

First published in Great Britain in 1972 by arrangement with
Cooper Square Inc. © Phyllis J. Walker, 1972.
Reprinted June 1972.

TUTANKHAMEN'S TREASURE

is an abridged edition of Howard Carter's three volume work,
The Tomb of Tutankhamen, which was first published by
instalments in 1923, 1927 and 1933 respectively.
A one volume edition of *The Tomb of Tutankhamen* is available
from Sphere Books in paperback and Barrie and Jenkins Ltd. in
hardcover. The text is unabridged, but the introductions and the
longer appendices have been omitted.

ILLUSTRATIONS

The black and white photographs were taken at the time of
excavation by the expedition's official photographer, Harry
Burton, who was on the staff of the Metropolitan Museum of Art,
New York. They are reproduced here by kind permission of the
Griffiths Institute, Ashmolean Museum, Oxford.
Acknowledgements for the colour plates are due to:

Plates 1, 2 and 4, photographs by F. L. Kennett
© copyright George Rainbird Ltd.
Plate 3, Scala.

TRADE
MARK

Printed in Great Britain by
Hazell Watson & Viney Ltd,
Aylesbury, Bucks

CONTENTS

LIST OF ILLUSTRATIONS

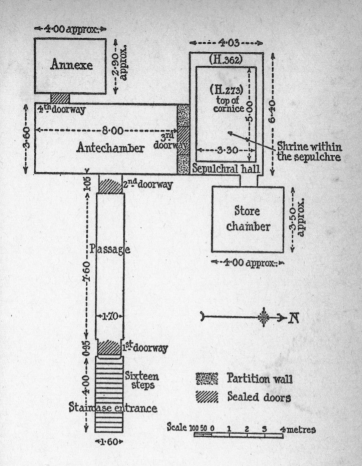

Plan of Tutankhamen's tomb

CHAPTER ONE

THE KING

Everyone knows the name of Tutankhamen, but his personality is still as elusive and tantalizing as a puzzle with missing pieces. We know that he was the son-in-law of the heretic king Akhenaten, but we still do not know whom his own parents were. He might have been born of the blood royal and have had some claim to the throne of Egypt in his own right. But on the other hand he might have been just an ordinary person. But when he married Akhenaten's daughter Ankhesenpaaten he at once became a potential heir to the throne by the Egyptian law of succession. We do not even know for certain when the marriage took place, but the princess Ankhesenpaaten cannot have been much more than ten years old at the time, and Tutankhamen himself was scarcely more than a boy.

The throne of Egypt then was a hazardous and uncomfortable place. Dissatisfaction was rife during the last years of Akhenaten's reign. The priests of the old religion had seen their gods flouted and discarded and their own livelihood threatened : the soldiers unused to being inactive were seething with discontent and ready for any form of excitement : the foreign 'harim' women who had come to the Court and into the families of the soldiers during the wars of conquest were now a centre for intrigue and plotting : the manufacturers and merchants were becoming sullen and discontented as their foreign trade declined, and the common people, resentful and bewildered at having lost their old gods were restless and uncertain.

So ruling Egypt was a difficult task for a young boy king when, in about 1362 BC Tutankhamen came to the throne, and we can be reasonably certain that Ay—

Chief Priest, Court Chamberlain and practically Court everything else was the real power behind the young king's throne. Ay had been a close personal friend of Akhenaten's and, if we look ahead a little, we see that he secured the throne for himself after Tutankhamen's death.

But what do we know about the boy king himself? Before we opened the inner chambers of the tomb we knew hardly anything—a few facts about his short reign comprised a niggardly total. We knew that at some point he abandoned the heretic capital of his father-in-law at Tell el Amarna and moved the court back to Thebes. We knew that he began as an Aten worshipper and reverted to the old religion of Amen because he changed his name from Tutankhaten to Tutankhamen, and his young bride changed hers from Ankhesenpaaten to Ankhesenamen, and because he made some additions and restorations to the temples of the old gods at Thebes. We knew, too, that some of the tribes of Syria and the Sudan were subject to him and brought him tribute, and on many objects in the outer chamber of his tomb we see him trampling with great gusto on prisoners of war, shooting them by the hundred from his chariot. But this did not mean that Tutankhamen went to the field of war himself for Egyptian monarchs were susceptible to such forms of flattering artistic license.

It was from the inner chambers of the tomb that we had to learn everything about the boy pharaoh : the length of his reign, how old was he when he died, and why did he die? Was it an accident, was he poisoned or killed some other way, or did he suffer from some incurable illness? These were points of paramount interest, but we hoped to learn much, much more in our search for the real king.

CHAPTER TWO

THE VALLEY AND THE TOMB

The Valley of the Tombs of the Kings—the name is
full of romance, and of all the wonders of Egypt it is
the most thrilling to the imagination. Here, in this
lonely valley head, far from every sound of life, guarded
by the "Horn", the highest peak in the Theban hills,
which towers like a natural pyramid above, lay buried
thirty or more Egyptian kings, amongst them the greatest Egypt ever knew.

Tucked away in a corner at the far end of the Valley,
half hidden by a projecting basin of rock, lies the entrance to the unostentatious tomb of Thothmes the
First.

This tomb is especially interesting for two reasons:
it was the first ever constructed in the Valley, and it
was also the first experiment in a new theory of tomb
design.

To the Egyptian it was a matter of extreme importance that his body should rest undisturbed in the place
built for it and earlier kings tried to insure this by erecting a mountain of stone over each tomb. It was essential
that the dead king, now called a mummy, should have
with him everything that he could possibly need, and
if he was a monarch who relished display and gorgeous
luxury, gold and treasures were buried with him. The
result is obvious. Within a few generations at most the
mummy would be disturbed by robbers who ransacked
the tomb's lavish wealth.

Various expedients were tried to protect the tomb:
the entrance passage—naturally the weak spot—was
plugged with granite monoliths weighing many tons;
false passages were constructed; secret doors contrived;
everything that ingenuity could suggest or wealth could

purchase was employed. Vain labour, for by patience and perseverance the tomb robber surmounted the difficulties set to baffle him. Moreover, the success of these expedients, and the safety of the tomb itself, was largely dependent on the good will of the mason who carried out the work and the architect who designed it, and, in private tombs at any rate, an entrance for plunderers was sometimes contrived by the officials who planned the work.

At the beginning of the Eighteenth Dynasty (about 1600 years BC) there was hardly a king's tomb in the whole of Egypt that had not been rifled—a somewhat grisly thought to the monarch who was choosing the site for his own last resting place. Thothmes I evidently found it so, and devoted a good deal of thought to the problem. He decided on secrecy as the one chance of escaping the fate of his predecessors, and as a result built the lonely little tomb at the head of the Valley.

The early funerary monuments always had near them a temple in which ceremonies were performed at various yearly festivals. Thothmes I decided there was to be no monument over the tomb itself, and the funerary temple in which the offerings were made was to be situated a mile or so away. It was certainly not a convenient arrangement, but it was necessary if the secrecy of the tomb was to be kept.

How long the secret of the tomb of Thothmes I held we do not know. Probably not long, for what secret was ever kept in Egypt? At the time of its discovery in 1899 little remained in it but the massive stone sarcophagus. The king himself had been moved, first of all to the tomb of his daughter Hatshepsut, and subsequently with other royal mummies to Deir el-Bahari. In any case, whether the hiding of the tomb was temporarily successful or not, a new fashion had been set, and the remaining kings of the Eighteenth Dynasty, together with those of the Nineteenth and Twentieth, were all buried in the Valley.

For a few generations, under the powerful kings of

the Eighteenth and Nineteenth dynasties, the Valley tombs must have been reasonably secure. In the Twentieth Dynasty it was quite another story. There were weaklings on the throne, cemetery guardians became lax and venial, and a regular orgy of grave robbing seems to have set in.

Strange sights the Valley must have seen, and desperate the ventures that took place in it. One can imagine the plotting for days beforehand, the secret rendezvous on the cliff by night, the bribing or drugging of the cemetery guards, and then the desperate burrowing in the dark, the scramble through a small hole into the burial chamber, the hectic search by a glimmering light for treasure that was portable, and the return home at dawn laden with booty. We can imagine these things, and at the same time realize how inevitable it all was. The temptation was too great. Wealth beyond the dreams of avarice lay there at the disposal of whoever should find the means to reach it, and sooner or later the tomb robber was bound to win.

By the Twenty-first Dynasty, all attempts at guarding the tombs seem to have been abandoned, and the royal mummies were moved about from sepulchre to sepulchre in a desperate effort to preserve them. No fewer than thirteen of the royal mummies were moved at one time or another to the tomb of Amenhetep II, and here they were allowed to remain. Other kings were eventually collected from their various hiding places, taken out of the Valley altogether, and placed in a well-hidden tomb cut in the Deir el-Bahari cliff. This was the final move, for by some accident the exact locality of the tomb was lost, and the mummies remained in peace for nearly three thousand years.

Throughout all these troubled times in the Twentieth and Twenty-first dynasties there is no mention of Tutankhamen and his tomb. He had not escaped altogether —his tomb having been entered within a very few years of his death—but he was lucky enough to escape the ruthless plundering of the later period. For some reason his tomb had been overlooked. It was situated in a very low-lying part of the Valley, and a heavy rainstorm might well have washed away all trace of its entrance. Or it may owe its safety to the fact that a number of huts, for use of workmen who were employed in excavating the tomb of a later king, were built immediately above it.

With the passing of the mummies the history of the Valley, as known to us from ancient Egyptian sources, comes to an end. Five hundred years had passed since Thothmes I constructed his modest little tomb there.

From now on we are to imagine a deserted valley, spirit-haunted, doubtless, to the Egyptian, its cavernous galleries plundered and empty, the entrances of many of them open, to become the home of fox, desert owl, or colonies of bats.

CHAPTER THREE

THE VALLEY IN MODERN TIMES

Let us now pass on to 1815. One of the most remarkable men in the whole history of Egyptology, a young Italian giant, Giovanni Battista Belzoni, spent five years in Egypt, excavating and collecting antiquities. He discovered and cleared a number of tombs in the Valley, including those of Ay, Mentuherkhepeshef, Rameses I, and Seti I. This was the first occasion on which excavations on a large scale had ever been made in the Valley. Belzoni, like everyone else who has ever dug in the Valley, thought that he had absolutely exhausted its possibilities.

But in 1844 the great German expedition under Karl Richard Lepsius made a complete survey of the Valley and cleared the tomb of Rameses II. Nothing more of any consequence was done in the Valley until the very end of the century.

In this period, however, just outside the Valley there occurred one of the most important events in the whole of its history. The various royal mummies had been collected from their hiding places and deposited all together in a rock cleft at Deir el-Bahari, where their rested for nearly three thousand years, and where, in the summer of 1875, they were found by the members of a family in the village of Kurna, the Abd-el-Rasuls. It was in the thirteenth century BC that the inhabitants of this village first adopted the trade of tomb-robbing, and it is a trade that they have adhered to steadfastly ever since.

On this occasion the find was too big to handle. It was obviously impossible to clear the tomb of its contents, so the whole family was sworn to secrecy, and determined to leave the find where it was, and to draw on it from time to time as they needed money. Incredible as it may seem the secret was kept for six years, and the family, with a banking account of forty or more dead pharaohs to draw upon, grew rich.

It soon became clear, from objects which came into the market, that there had been a rich find of royal material somewhere, but it was not until 1881 that it was possible to trace the sale of the objects to the Adb-el-Rasul family. One of them made a full confession. News was telegraphed at once to Cairo, Emile Brugsch Bey of the Cairo Museum was sent up to investigate and take charge, and on the fifth of July, 1881, the long-kept secret was revealed to him. It must have been an amazing experience. There, huddled together in a shallow, ill-cut grave, lay the most powerful monarchs of the ancient East, kings whose names were familiar to the whole world, whom no one in his wildest moments had ever dreamed of seeing. The kings were embarked upon the museum barge; and within fifteen days of Brugsch Bey's arrival at the Valley they were landed in Cairo and deposited in the museum.

In 1898, acting on information supplied by local officials, Victor Loret, then Director General of the Service of Antiquities, opened up several new royal tombs in the Valley, including those of Thothmes I, Thothmes III, and Amenhetep II. This last was a very important discovery. In the Twenty-first Dynasty thirteen royal mummies had found sanctuary in Amenhetep's tomb and here, in 1898, the thirteen were found. It was but their mummies that remained. The wealth had long since vanished.

The body of Amenhetep still lay within its own sarcophagus, where it had rested for more than three thousand years. The Egyptian government decided against its removal. The tomb was barred and bolted, a guard was placed upon it, and there the king was left in peace.

In 1902 permission to dig in the Valley under supervision of the Egyptian government was granted to an American, Theodore Davis, and he subsequently excavated there for twelve consecutive seasons. His principal finds included the tombs of Thothmes IV, Hatshepsut, SoPtah, Yua and Thua (great-grandfather and grand-mother of Tutankhamen's queen), Horemheb, and a vault, not a real tomb, devised for the transfer of the burial of Akhenaten from its original tomb at Tell el-Amarna. This cache included the mummy and coffin of Akhenaten, a very small part of his funerary equip-ment, and portions of the sepulchral shrine of his mother, Tyi. In 1914 we acquired Mr. Davis's con-cession, and the story of the tomb of Tutankhamen really begins.

CHAPTER FOUR

WE BEGIN WORK AT THEBES

Theodore Davis had decided that the Valley was exhausted, and that there were no more tombs to be found. Nevertheless he was loath to give up the site, and it was not until June, 1914, that Lord Carnarvon and I actually received the long-coveted concession. Sir Gaston Maspero, Director of the Antiquities Department, who signed our concession, agreed with Mr. Davis that the site was exhausted.

We had made a thorough investigation of the site, and were quite sure that there were areas, covered by the dumps of previous excavators, which had never been properly examined. At the risk of being accused of hindsight, I will state that we had definite hopes of finding the tomb of one particular king, that of Tutankhamen.

This belief is explained by the published record of Mr. Davis's excavations. Towards the end of his work in the Valley he had found, hidden under a rock, a faience cup which bore the name of Tutankhamen. In the same region he came upon a small pit tomb, in which were fragments of gold foil, bearing the figures and names of Tutankhamen and his queen. On the basis of these fragments of gold he claimed that he had actually found the burial place of Tutankhamen. The theory was quite untenable, for the pit tomb in question was small and insignificant, ludicrously inadequate for a king's burial in the Eighteenth Dynasty. Some little distance eastward from this tomb, he had also found, buried in an irregular hole cut in the side of the rock, a cache of large pottery jars, with sealed mouths and hieratic inscriptions. A brief examination was made of their contents, which seemed to consist of broken pottery, bundles of linen, and other oddments. Mr. Davis refused to be interested in them. The entire collection of jars was sent to the Metropolitan Museum of Art in New York. They proved extraordinarily interesting. There were clay seals, some bearing the name of Tutankhamen and others the impression of the Royal Necropolis Seal, fragments of magnificent painted pottery vases, linen head shawls—one inscribed with the latest known date of Tutankhamen's reign—floral collars of the kind represented as worn by mourners in burial scenes, and a mass if other miscellaneous objects; the whole apparently representing the material which had been used during the funeral ceremonies of Tutankhamen, afterwards gathered together and stacked away within the jars.

We had thus three distinct pieces of evidence which seemed to connect Tutankhamen with this particular part of the Valley. To these must be added a fourth. It was in close to these other finds that Mr. Davis had discovered the famous Akhenaten cache. This contained the funerary remains of heretic members of the royal family, brought hurriedly and hidden here for safety, and we can be reasonably sure that Tutankhamen was responsible for their removal and reburial because a number of his clay seals were found.

With all this evidence we were thoroughly convinced that the tomb of Tutankhamen was still to be found, and that it ought to be situated not far from the centre of the Valley. We were in the act of completing our plans for an elaborate campaign in the seasons of 1914–1915 when war broke out, and for the time being all our plans had to be abandoned.

We resumed our work in this region in the season of 1919–1920. The idea was to clear the whole remaining part of the triangle of ground defined by the tombs of Rameses II, Merenptah, and Rameses IV—the area in which we hoped the tomb of Tutankhamen might be situated—and we started in with a fairly large gang of workmen. By the time Lord and Lady Carnarvon arrived in March the top debris had been removed, and we were ready to clear down into what we believed to be virgin ground below. We soon had proof that we were right, for we came upon a small cache containing thirteen alabaster jars, bearing the names of Rameses II and Merenptah, probably from the tomb of the latter. As this was the nearest approach to a real find that we had yet made in the Valley, we were naturally excited, and Lady Carnarvon, I remember, insisted on digging out these jars—they were beautiful specimens—with her own hands.

With the exception of the ground covered by the workmen's huts, we had now exhausted the whole triangular area and had found no tomb. For our next attempt we selected the small valley in which the tomb of Thothmes III was situated. This occupied us throughout the whole of the two following seasons. Nothing intrinsically valuable was found.

We had now dug in the Valley for several seasons with extremely scanty results, and it became a much debated question whether we should continue the work or try for a more profitable site elsewhere. After these barren years were we justified in going on with it? My own feeling was that so long as a single area of untouched ground remained, the risk was worth taking. There was still the combination of flint boulders and workmen's huts at the foot of the tomb of Rameses VI to be investigated, and I had always had a kind of superstitious feeling that in that particular corner of the Valley one of the missing kings, possibly Tutankhamen, might be found. Certainly the stratification of the debris there could indicate a tomb. Eventually we decided to devote one final season to the Valley.

CHAPTER FIVE

FINDING THE TOMB

And so we began the final season in the Valley. We had excavated there for six full seasons, and season after season had drawn a blank; we had worked for months at a stretch and found nothing, and only an excavator knows how desperately depressing that can be. We had almost made up our minds that we were beaten, and were preparing to leave the Valley and try our luck elsewhere; and then, hardly had we set hoe to ground in our last despairing effort, than we made a discovery that far exceeded our wildest dreams. Surely, never before in the whole history of excavation has a full digging season been compressed within the space of five days.

Let me try and tell the story of it all. I arrived in Luxor on October 28 (1922) and by November 1st had enrolled my workmen and was ready to begin. Our former excavations had stopped short at the northeast corner of the tomb of Rameses VI, and from this point I started trenching southward. In this area there were a number of roughly constructed workmen's huts, used probably by the labourers in the tomb of Rameses. These huts, built about three feet above bedrock, covered the whole area in front of the Rameses side tomb and continued in a southerly direction to join up with a similar group of huts on the opposite side of the Valley. By the evening of November 3rd, we had uncovered a sufficient number of these huts for experimental purposes, so, after we had noted them, they were removed, and we were ready to clear away the three feet of soil that lay beneath them.

Hardly had I arrived next morning than the unusual silence, due to the stoppage of work, made me realize that something out of the ordinary had happened, and I was greeted by the announcement that a step cut in the rock had been discovered underneath the very first hut to be attacked. This seemed too good to be true, but a short amount of extra clearing revealed the fact that we were actually in the entrance of a steep cut in the rock, some thirteen feet below the entrance to the tomb of Rameses VI, and a similar depth from the present bed level of the Valley. The manner of cutting was that of the sunken stairway entrance so common in the Valley, and I almost dared to hope that we had found our tomb at last. Work continued feverishly throughout the whole of that day and the morning of the next, but it was not until the following afternoon that we succeeded in clearing away the masses of rubbish and were able to demarcate the upper edges of that stairway on all its four sides.

It was clear by now beyond any question that we actually had before us the entrance to a tomb, but there was always the horrible possibility that the tomb was an unfinished one, never completed and never used; if it had been finished there was the depressing possibility that it had been completely plundered in ancient times. On the other hand, there was just the chance of an untouched or only partially plundered tomb, and it was with great excitement that I watched the descending steps of the staircase as they came to light. Work progressed more rapidly now; step succeeded step, and at the level of the twelfth, towards sunset, there was disclosed the upper part of a doorway : blocked, plastered, and sealed.

A sealed doorway—it was actually true, then ! Our years of patient labour were to be rewarded after all. With excitement growing to fever heat I searched the seal impressions on the door for evidence of the identity of the owner, but could find no name : the only decipherable ones were those of the Royal Necropolis Seal. Two facts were clear : first, the use of this royal seal was certain evidence that the tomb had been built for a person of very high standing; and second, that the sealed door was entirely screened from above by workmen's huts of the Twentieth Dynasty was sufficient proof that at least from that date it had never been entered.

While examining the seals I noted, at the top of the doorway where some of the plaster had fallen away, a heavy wooden lintel. Under this, to assure myself of the method by which the doorway had been blocked, I made a small peephole, just large enough to insert an electric torch, and discovered that the passage beyond the door was filled completely from floor to ceiling with stones and rubble—additional proof of the care with which the tomb had been protected.

It was a thrilling moment. Anything, literally anything, might lie beyond that passage, and I needed all my self-control to keep from breaking down the doorway and investigating then and there.

One thing puzzled me, and that was the smallness of the opening in comparison with the ordinary Valley tombs. The design was certainly of the Eighteenth Dynasty. Could it be the tomb of a noble buried here by royal consent or was it a royal cache, a hiding place to which a mummy and its equipment had been removed for safety? Or was it actually the tomb of the king for whom I had spent so many years in search?

Naturally my wish was to go straight ahead with our clearing, to find out the full extent of the discovery, but Lord Carnarvon was in England and in fairness to him I had to delay matters until he could come.

My next task was to secure the doorway against interference until it could finally be reopened. This we did by filling our excavation up again to surface level, and rolling on top of it the large flint boulders of which the workmen's huts had been composed. By the evening, exactly forty-eight hours after we had discovered the first step of the staircase, the tomb had vanished. So far as the appearance of the ground was concerned there had never been any tomb, and I found it hard at times to persuade myself that the whole episode had not been a dream.

But news travels fast in Egypt, and without two days of the discovery congratulations, inquiries, and offers of help descended upon me from all directions. It became clear that I was in for a job that could not be tackled singlehanded, so I wired to A. R. Callender, who had helped me on previous occasions, asking him, if possible, to join me without delay, and to my relief he arrived the very next day.

On November 8th I had received a message from Lord Carnarvon, which read, "Propose arrive Alexandria twentieth."

On the night of November 18th I went to Cairo, returning to Luxor on the 21st. On the 23rd, Lord Carnarvon arrived in Luxor with his daughter, Lady Evelyn Herbert, his devoted companion in all his Egyptian work, and everything was ready for the beginning of the second chapter of the discovery of the tomb.

By the afternoon of the 24th the whole staircase was clear, sixteen steps in all, and we were able to make a proper examination of the sealed doorway. On the lower part the seal impressions were much clearer, and we were able without much difficulty to make out on several of them the name of Tutankhamen.

With heightened interest we renewed our investigation of the doorway. Here a disquieting element made its appearance. Now that the whole door was exposed to light it was possible to discern a fact that had escaped notice—there had been two successive openings and reclosings of a part of its surface. Furthermore the Royal Necropolis Seal originally discovered had been applied to the reclosed portions, whereas the sealings of Tutankhamen covered the untouched part of the doorway and were therefore those with which the tomb had been originally secured. The tomb then was not absolutely intact, as we had hoped. Plunderers had entered it, and entered it more than once—but that they had not rifled it completely was evident from that fact that it had been resealed.

Then came another puzzle. In the lower strata of rubbish that filled the staircase we found masses of broken potsherds and boxes bearing the name of Akhenaten, SmenkhkaRe, and Tutankhamen, and, what was much more upsetting, a scarab of Thothmes III and a fragment with the name of Amenhetep III. Why this mixture of names? The balance of evidence so far would seem to indicate a cache rather than a tomb, and at this stage we inclined more and more to the opinion that we were about to find a miscellaneous collection of objects of the Eighteenth Dynasty kings, brought from Tell el Amarna by Tutankhamen, and deposited here for safety.

So matters stood on the evening of November 24th. On the following day the sealed doorway was to be removed so Callender set carpenters to work making a heavy wooden grille to be set up in its place. On the morning of the 25th the seal impressions on the doorways were carefully noted and photographed, and then we removed the actual blocking of the door, consisting of rough stones carefully built from floor to lintel and heavily plastered on their outer faces to take the seal impressions.

This disclosed the beginning of a descending passage, the same width as the entrance stairway, and nearly seven feet high. As I had already discovered from my hole in the doorway, it was filled completely with stone and rubble, probably the chip from its own excavation. This filling, like the doorway, showed distinct signs of more than one opening and reclosing of the tomb, the untouched part consisting of clean white chip, mingled with dust; whereas the disturbed part was composed mainly of dark flint. It was clear that an irregular tunnel had been cut through the original filling at the upper corner on the left side, a tunnel corresponding in position to the hole in the doorway.

The following day was the day of days, the most

wonderful that I have ever lived through, whose like I could never hope to see again. Throughout the morning the work of clearing continued, slowly, on account of the delicate objects that were mixed with the filling. Then, in the middle of the afternoon, thirty feet down from the outer door, we came upon a second sealed doorway, almost an exact replica of the first. The seal impressions in this case were less distinct, but still recognizable as those of Tutankhamen and of the royal necropolis. Here again the signs of opening and reclosing were clearly marked upon the plaster. We were firmly convinced by this time that it was a cache that we were about to open, and not a tomb. We were soon to know. There lay the sealed doorway, and behind it was the answer to the question.

Slowly, desperately slowly it seemed to us as we watched, the debris that encumbered the lower part of the doorway was removed, until at last we had the whole door clear before us. With trembling hands I made a tiny breach in the upper-left-hand corner. Darkness and blank space, as far as an iron testing rod could reach, showed that whatever lay beyond was empty. Candle tests were applied as a precaution against possible foul gases, and then, widening the hole a little, I inserted the candle and peered in, Lord Carnarvon, Lady Evelyn, and Callender standing anxiously beside me to hear the verdict. At first I could see nothing—the hot air escaping from the chamber caused the candle flame to flicker—but presently, as my eyes grew accustomed to the light, details of the room within emerged slowly from the mist : strange animals, statues, and gold—everywhere the glint of gold. For the moment—an eternity it must have seemed to the others —I was struck dumb with amazement, and when Lord Carnarvon, unable to stand the suspense any longer, inquired anxiously, "Can you see anything?" it was all I could do to get out the words, "Yes, wonderful things."

CHAPTER SIX

A PRELIMINARY INVESTIGATION

Never before in the whole history of excavation had such an amazing sight been seen. Imagine how the objects in the tomb appeared to us as we looked down upon them from our spy hole in the doorway, casting our beam of torch light from one group of objects to another, in a vain attempt to interpret the treasure that lay before us. The effect was bewildering, overwhelming. We had never dreamed of anything like this, a roomful—a whole museumful it seemed—of objects, some familiar, but some the like of which we had never seen, piled one upon another in seemingly endless profusion.

Gradually the scene grew clearer, and we could pick out individual objects. First, opposite to us—we had been conscious of them all the while, but refused to believe in them—were three great gilt couches, their sides carved in the form of monstrous animals, curiously attenuated in body, as they had to be to serve their purpose, but with heads of startling realism. Uncanny beasts to look upon; as we saw them, their brilliant gilded surfaces picked out of the darkness by our electric torch, as though by limelight, their heads throwing grotesque distorted shadows on the wall behind them, they were almost terrifying. Next, on the right, two statues held our attention : lifesized figures of kings in black, facing each other like sentinels, black, gold-kilted, gold-sandaled, armed with mace and staff, the protective sacred cobras upon their foreheads. Between them, around them, piled on top of them, were countless other objects—exquisitely painted and inlaid caskets ; alabaster vases, some beautifully carved in openwork designs ; strange black shrines, a great gilt snake peeping out from the open door of one; bouquets of flowers or leaves; beds; beautifully carved chairs; a golden inlaid throne; a heap of curious white egg-shaped boxes; staves of all shapes and designs; beneath us, on the very threshhold of the chamber, a beautiful lotus-shaped cup of translucent alabaster; on the left a confused pile of overturned chariots, glistening with gold and inlay; and peeping from behind them another portrait of a king.

Such were some of the treasures that lay before us. Presently it dawned upon our bewildered brains that in all this medley of objects there was no coffin, no trace of mummy, and the much-debated question of tomb or cache began to intrigue us afresh. We re-examined the scene before us and noticed for the first time that between the two black sentinel statues on the right there was another sealed doorway. The explanation gradually dawned upon us. We were merely on the threshhold of our discovery. What we saw was just an ante-chamber. Behind the guarded door there were other chambers, possibly a succession of them, and in one of them, beyond any shadow of a doubt, in all his magnificent array of death, we should find the pharaoh lying.

We reclosed the hole, locked the wooden grille that had been placed upon the first doorway, left our guard, mounted our donkeys, and rode down the Valley, strangely silent and subdued.

It was curious, as we talked things over in the evening, to find how conflicting our ideas were about what we had seen. Each of us had noticed something that the others had not, and it amazed us next day to discover how many obvious things we had missed. Naturally, it was the sealed door between the statues that intrigued us most, and we debated far into the night the possibilities of what might lie behind it. A single chamber with the king's sarcophagus? That was the least we might expect. But why one chamber only? Why not a succession of passages and chambers, leading, in true Valley style, to an innermost shrine of all, the burial chamber? It might be so, and yet in plan the tomb was quite unlike the others. Visions of chamber after chamber, each crowded with objects like the one we had seen, passed through our minds. Then came the thought of the plunderers. Had they succeeded in penetrating this third doorway—seen from a distance it looked absolutely untouched—and, if so, what were our chances of finding the king's mummy intact? We slept little that night.

Next morning there was much to be done. It was essential to have some more adequate means of illumination before proceeding. Meanwhile we made careful notes of the seal impressions upon the inner doorways and then removed its entire blocking. By noon everything was ready and Lord Carnarvon, Lady Evelyn, Callender, and I entered the tomb and made a careful inspection of the first chamber, the Antechamber.

By the aid of the powerful electric lamps many things that had been obscure on the previous day became clear, and we were able to make a more accurate estimate of the extent of our discovery. Our first objective was naturally the sealed door between the statues, and here a disappointment awaited us. Seen from a distance it presented all the appearance of an absolutely intact blocking, but close examination revealed the fact that a small breach had been made near the bottom, just wide enough to admit a boy or a slightly built man, and that the hole had subsequently been filled up and resealed. We were not to be the first. Here, too, the thieves had forestalled us. It only remained to be seen how much damage they had done.

Our natural impulse was to break down the door, and get to the bottom of the matter at once, but to do so would have entailed serious risk of damage to many of the objects in the Antechamber, a risk which we were not prepared to take. Nor could we move anything for it was imperative that a plan and complete photographic record should be made before anything was touched, and this was a task involving a considerable amount of time, and equipment. Reluctantly we decided to abandon the opening of this inner sealed door until we had cleared the Antechamber of all of its contents. By doing this we should not only insure the complete scientific record of the outer chamber which it was our duty to make, but we should have a clear field for the removal of the door-blocking, a ticklish operation at best.

Having satisfied our curiosity about the sealed doorway, we could now turn our attention to the rest of the chamber, and make a more detailed examination of the objects which it contained. It was certainly an astounding experience. Here, packed tightly together, were scores of objects, any one of which would have filled us with excitement under ordinary circumstances. Some were of types well enough known to us; others were new and strange, and in some cases these were complete and perfect examples of objects whose appearance we had previously guessed at from the evidence of tiny broken fragments found in other royal tombs.

Nor was it merely in quantity that the find was so amazing. The period to which the tomb belongs is in many respects the most interesting in the whole history of Egyptian art, and we were prepared for beautiful things. What we were not prepared for was the astonishing vitality and animation which characterized certain of the objects. It was a revelation of unsuspected possibilities in Egyptian art, and we realized, even in this hasty preliminary survey, that a study of the material would involve a modification, if not a complete revolution, of all our old ideas.

One of the first things we noted in our survey was that all of the larger objects, and most of the smaller ones, were inscribed with the name of Tutankhamen. His, too, were the seals upon the innermost door, and therefore his, beyond any shadow of doubt, the mummy that ought to lie behind it. Next came a new discovery. Peering beneath the southernmost of the three great couches we noticed a small irregular hole in the wall.

Here was yet another sealed doorway, and a plunderer's hole, which, unlike the others, had never been repaired. Cautiously we crept under the couch, inserted our portable light, and there before us lay another chamber, rather smaller than the first, but even more crowded with objects.

The state of this inner room simply defied description. In the Antechamber there had been some sort of an attempt to tidy up after the plunderers' visit, but here everything was in confusion, just as they had left it. Nor did it take much imagination to picture them at their work. One—there would probably not have been room for more—had crept into the chamber, and had then hastily but systematically ransacked its entire contents, emptying boxes, throwing things aside, piling them one upon another, and occasionally passing objects through the hole to his companions. He had done his work just about as thoroughly as an earthquake. Not a single inch of floor space remained vacant. Beautiful things it contained, too, smaller than those in the Antechamber for the most part, but many of them of exquisite workmanship. Several things remain in my mind particularly—a painted box, quite as lovely as the one in the Antechamber; a wonderful chair of ivory, gold, wood, and leatherwork; alabaster and faience vases of beautiful form; and a gaming board, in carved and coloured ivory.

I think the discovery of this second chamber had a sobering effect upon us. For the first time we began to realize what a prodigious task we had in front of us, and what a responsibility it entailed. The find was unprecedented, and for the moment it seemed as though there were more to be done than any human being could accomplish.

Moreover, the extent of our discovery had taken us by surprise, and we were wholly unprepared to deal with the multitude of objects that lay before us, many in a perishable condition and needing careful preservative treatment before they could be touched. There were countless things to be done before we could even begin the work of clearing. Vast stores of preservatives and packing material had to be laid in; expert advice was needed as to the best method of dealing with certain objects; provision must be made for a laboratory— some safe and sheltered spot in which the objects could be treated, catalogued, and packed—a careful scale plan had to be made and a complete photographic record taken while everything was still in position; a dark-room had to be contrived.

But the first thing to be done was to make the tomb secure against robbery; we could then work out our plans with easy minds. We had our wooden grille at the passage entrance, but that was not enough, and I measured the inner doorway for a gate of thick steel bars. Until we could get this made for us we must go to the labour of filling in the tomb once more.

On December 3rd, after closing up the entrance doorway with heavy timber, the tomb was filled to surface level. Lord Carnarvon and Lady Evelyn left on the 4th for England, to conclude various arrangements there, preparatory to returning later in the season; and on the 6th, leaving Callender to watch over the tomb, I went to Cairo to make my purchases. My first care was the steel gate, and I ordered it the morning I arrived, under promise that it should be delivered within six days. The other purchases I took more leisurely, photographic material, chemicals, a motor car, packing boxes of every kind, with thirty-two bales of calico, more than a mile of wadding, and as much again of surgical bandages.

While in Cairo I had time to take stock of the position, and it became more and more clear to me that assistance on a big scale was necessary if the work in the tomb was to be carried out in a satisfactory manner. I was extremely fortunate in gaining the assistance of Harry Burton, the photographic expert from the Egyptian Department of the Metropolitan Museum of Art in New York. The Metropolitan Museum also provided the skilled services of three others of its staff : Mr. Arthur C. Mace, director of the excavations on the pyramid field at Lisht, Mr. Hall and Mr. Hauser who were the draftsmen capable of making the scale drawings of the Antechamber and its contents. Another piece of luck befell me in Cairo when Mr. Lucas, Director of the Chemical Department of the Egyptian Government abandoned his own vacation plans and placed his knowledge at our disposal for three months, a generous offer which I hastened to accept.

With a highly qualified working team complete, I returned to Luxor and on December 16th we opened up the tomb once more. The next day the steel gate was set up in the door of the chamber and we were ready to begin work. On the 18th, work actually began, Burton making his first photographic experiments in the Antechamber, and Hall and Hauser starting on their plan. Two days later Lucas arrived, and at once began experimenting with preservatives for the various classes of objects.

On the 22nd, as the result of a good deal of clamour, permission was given to the press, both European and native, to see the tomb. On the 25th, Mace arrived, and two days later, photographs and plans being sufficiently advanced, the first object was removed from the tomb.

CHAPTER SEVEN

A SURVEY OF THE ANTECHAMBER

We made a detailed study of the objects in the Antechamber. This was a small room, some twenty-six by twelve feet, and we had to tread warily for a single false step or hasty movement would have inflicted irreparable damage on one of the delicate objects with which we were surrounded.

In front of us, in the doorway, lay the beautiful wishing cup. It was of pure semi-translucent alabaster, with lotus-flower handles on either side, supporting the kneeling figures which symbolize Eternity. Turning right as we entered, we noticed, first, a large cylindrical jar of alabaster; next, two funerary bouquets of leaves, one leaning against the wall, the other fallen; and in front of them, standing out in the chamber, a painted wooden casket. This last probably ranks as one of the greatest artistic treasures of the tomb. Its outer face was completely covered with gesso; upon this prepared surface there were a series of brilliantly coloured and exquisitely painted designs—hunting scenes upon the curved panels of the lid, battle scenes upon the sides, and upon the ends representations of the king in the shape of a lion, trampling his enemies underfoot. This was the first casket we opened, and its contents were an odd assortment of sandals, decorated robes and beads, crushed and bundled together.

Next, we came to the end (north) wall of the chamber. Here was the tantalising sealed doorway, and on either side of it, mounting guard over the entrance, stood the life-size wooden statues of the king, strange and imposing.

Turning now to the long (west) wall of the chamber, we found the whole of the wall-space occupied by the three great animal-sided couches, curious pieces of furniture which we knew from illustrations in tomb paintings, but of which we had never seen actual examples. The first was lion-headed; the second cow-headed, and the third had the head of a composite animal, half hippopotamus and half crocodile. Each was made in four pieces for convenience in carrying, the actual bed frame fitting by means of hook and staple to the animals' sides, the animals' feet fitting into an open pedestal. As is usually the case in Egyptian beds, each had a foot panel but nothing at the head.

Beneath the lion-headed couch, resting on the floor, stood a large chest, made of a delightful combination of ebony, ivory, and redwood, which contained a number of small vases of alabaster and glass; two black wooden shrines, each containing a gilt figure of a snake, emblem and standard of the tenth province of Upper Egypt; a little chair, too small for other than a child's use; two folding duck-stools, inlaid with ivory; and an alabaster box, with incised ornamentation filled in with pigments.

Standing on the floor in front of the cow-headed couch were two wooden boxes. Thrown carelessly in were a number of faience cups, boomerangs mounted at either end with blue faience; a very elaborate tapestry-woven garment; and the greater part of a corselet. This last was composed of several thousand pieces of gold, glass, and faience. Below the couch, a pile of egg-shaped wooden cases contained trussed ducks and other food offerings.

The third couch was flanked by its pair of queer composite animals, with open mouths, and teeth and tongues of ivory. Below this couch stood another of the great artistic treasures of the tomb, a throne, overlaid with gold from top to bottom, and richly adorned with glass, faience, and stone inlay. Its legs, fashioned in feline form, were surmounted by lions' heads, fascinating in their strength and simplicity. Magnificent crowned and winged serpents formed the arms, and between the bars which supported the back were six protective cobras, carved in wood, gilded, and inlaid. It was the panel of the back, however, that was the chief glory of the throne, and I had no hesitation in claiming that it was the most beautiful thing that had yet been found in Egypt.

The scenes on the panel show one of the halls of the palace, a room decorated with flower-garlanded pillars, frieze of royal cobras, and dado of conventional "recessed" panelling. The king himself sits in an unconventional attitude upon a cushioned throne, his arm thrown carelessly across its back. Before him stands the girlish figure of the queen, apparently putting the last touches to his toilet : in one hand she holds a small jar of scent or ointment, and with the other she gently anoints his shoulder or adds a touch of perfume to his collar.

The colouring of the panel is extraordinarily vivid and effective. The face and other exposed portions of the bodies both of king and queen are of red glass, and the head-dresses of brilliant turquoise-like faience. The robes are of silver, dulled by age to an exquisite bloom. The background is the sheet gold with which the throne was covered. In its original state, with gold and silver fresh and new, the throne must have been an almost too dazzling sight : now, toned down a little by the tarnishing of the alloy, it presents a colour scheme that is extraordinarily atractive and harmonious.

Apart from its artistic merit, the throne is an important historical document : the scenes upon it being actual illustrations of the political and religious events of the reign.

The rest of the south wall and the whole of the east, as far as the entrance doorway, were taken up by the parts of no fewer than four chariots. They were heaped together in terrible confusion, the plunderers having evidently turned them this way and that, in their endeavours to secure the more valuable portions of the gold decoration which covered them. Theirs not the

The Road to the Tomb of Kings

The Antechamber

The Chariots as they were found in the Antechamber

The sealed door between the statues

Anubis guarding the entrance to the innermost Treasury

Lord Carnarvon (left) and Howard Carter opening the door to the Sepulchral chamber

The oars placed between the outermost shrine and the wall of the **Burial Chamber**

whole responsibility, however. The entrance passage was far too narrow to admit the complete chariots, so to enable them to get into the chamber the axles were sawn in two, the wheels dismounted and piled together, and the dismembered bodies placed by themselves.

CHAPTER EIGHT

CLEARING THE ANTECHAMBER

It took us seven weeks to clear the Antechamber, and we were indeed thankful when we had finished without any kind of disaster occurring. Moving the objects was like playing a gigantic game of spillikins: it was extremely difficult to move one object without damaging others. Sometimes life was a nightmare—we were afraid to move lest we should kick against a prop and bring everything crashing down. Certain things were in beautiful condition, as strong as when they were first made; others could not be touched at all without preservative treatment being applied. It was slow work, painfully slow and terribly nerve-racking, and we constantly felt the full weight of our great responsibility.

The first object to be moved was the painted wooden casket. Then, working from north to south we gradually cleared the great animal couches. Each object was placed upon a padded wooden stretcher and fastened securely to it with bandages. From time to time, when enough stretchers had been filled—on average this was once a day—a convoy was made up and dispatched under guard to the laboratory.

Moving and transporting the smaller things was a comparatively simple matter. Not so when we came to move the great couches themselves. They must have been assembled in the tomb, and we had to dismantle them to get them out, no easy matter, for after three thousand years the bronze hooks had set tight in the staples and would not budge. We got them apart eventually with hardly any damage, but it took five of us to do it. The chariots were the most difficult of all to get out: Egyptian chariots are of a very light construction, and the rough usage afforded these had made them exceptionally delicate and hazardous to handle.

We had one big scare. For two or three days the sky was very black, and it looked as though we were in for one of the heavy storms that occasionally break over Thebes. Then the rain comes down in torrents, and the whole bed of the Valley becomes a raging flood. No power on earth could have prevented our tomb from being flooded if this had happened, but, fortunately, though there was heavy rain somewhere in the district, we escaped with only a few drops.

In the course of our clearing we naturally accumulated a good deal of evidence about the original tomb plunderers. In the first place, we know from the sealings on the outer doorway that all the plundering was done within a very few years of the king's burial. We also know that the plunderer entered the tomb at least twice. It is just possible that the first plundering was done immediately after the funeral ceremonies. Afterwards, the passage was entirely filled with stones and rubbish, and it was through a tunnel excavated in the upper-left-hand corner of this filling that subsequent attempts were made. At the final attempt the thieves had penetrated all the chambers of the tomb, but their tunnel was only a narrow one, and clearly they could not have got away with any except the smaller objects.

There was a strange difference between the state in which the Antechamber and the Annexe had been left. In the Annexe everything was in confusion, and there was not a vacant inch of floorspace. It was quite evident that the plunderers had turned everything topsy-turvy, and the present state of the chamber was precisely as they had left it. The Antechamber was quite different. There was a certain amount of confusion, but it was orderly confusion, and had it not been for the evidence afforded by the tunnel and the resealed doorways, one might have imagined at first view that there never had been any plundering, and that the confusion was due to carelessness at the time of the funeral.

However, when we commenced clearing it quickly

became clear that this comparative orderliness was due to a process of hasty tidying-up, and that the plunderers had been just as busy in the Antechamber as they had in the Annexe. Parts of the same object were found in different quarters of the chamber; objects that should have been in boxes were lying on the floor or upon the couches; there was a box lid behind the chariots, in an entirely inaccessible place, the box to which it belonged being far away, near the innermost door.

Later, when we came to unpack the boxes, we found still more circumstantial evidence. One long white box at the north end of the chamber was half full of sticks, bows, and arrows, and above, stuffed tightly in upon them, there was a mixed collection of the king's under-linen. Yet the metal points had been broken from all the arrows, and a few were found dropped on the floor. In another box, jewellery and tiny statuettes had been packed on top of faience libation vases. Others, again, were half empty, or contained a mere jumble of odds and ends of cloth. The confusion was due to hasty re-packing.

We could now reconstruct the whole sequence of events. A breach was first made in the upper-left-hand corner of the first sealed door, just large enough to admit a man, and then the tunnelling began, the excavators working in a chain, passing the stones and baskets of earth back from one to another. Seven or eight hours' work might suffice to bring them to the second sealed door; a hole in this, and they were through. Then in the semi-darkness began a mad scramble for loot. Gold was their natural quarry, but it had to be in portable form, and it must have maddened them to see it glinting all around them on plated objects which they could not move, and had no time to strip. Nor, in the dim light, could they always distinguish between the real and the false, and many an object which they took for solid gold was found on closer examination to be but gilded wood, and was contemptuously thrown aside. The boxes were treated in very drastic fashion. They were all dragged into the centre of the room and ransacked, their contents strewn all over the floor. What valuables the thieves found in them and made away with we may never know, but their search must have been hurried and superficial, for many objects of solid gold were overlooked. One very valuable thing they did secure. Within the small gold shrine there was a pedestal of gilded wood, made for a statuette, with the imprint of the statuette's feet still marked upon it. The statuette itself was gone and doubtless it had been a solid gold one.

When the Antechamber had been thoroughly worked over, the thieves turned their attention to the Annexe, knocking a hole in its doorway just big enough to let them through, and overturning and ransacking its contents quite as thoroughly as those of the Antechamber.

Then they directed their attentions towards the burial chamber, and made a very small hole in the sealed doorway which screened it from the Antechamber. They may, indeed, have been disturbed at this particular stage in the proceedings. A very interesting little piece of evidence seems to bear this theory out. In the Antechamber one of the boxes contained a handful of solid gold rings tied up in a fold of cloth. They were just the thing to attract a thief, for their intrinsic value was considerable, and yet they could easily be hidden. Now, every visitor to Egypt knows that if you give money to a *fellah* he would always undo a portion of his head shawl, put the coins in a fold of it, and finally secure it by looping the impromptu bag into a knot. This, unquestionably, was the work of one of the thieves. It was not his head shawl that he had used—the *fellah* of that period wore no such garment—but one of the king's scarves which he had picked up in the tomb, and he had fastened the coins thus for convenience in carrying. How, then, did it happen that the precious bundle of rings was left in the tomb and not carried off? It was the very last thing that a thief would be likely to forget, and, in the case of sudden alarm, it was not heavy enough to hinder his flight, however hurried that might be. We can conclude that the thieves were either trapped within the tomb, or overtaken in their flight—traced, in any case, with some of the plunder still upon them. This would explain the presence of certain other pieces of jewellery and goldwork too valuable to leave and too big to overlook.

In any case the fact that a robbery had been committed got to the ears of the officials, and they came to the tomb to investigate and make good the damage. For some reason they seem to have been in almost as great a hurry as the thieves, and their repairs were sadly inadequate. The Annexe they left severely alone, not even taking the trouble to fill up the hole in the doorway. In the Antechamber the smaller objects with which the floor was covered were swept up, bundled together, and jammed back into the boxes, no attempt being made to sort the material, or to put the objects into the boxes for which they had been originally intended. Some of the boxes were packed tight, others were left almost empty. Nor was all the small material even gathered up. The larger objects were pushed carelessly back against the walls, or stacked one upon another. Certainly no respect was shown, either to the objects themselves or to the king whose property they were, and we wondered why, if they tidied up so badly, they took the trouble to tidy up at all. One thing we must credit them with : they did not do any pilfering as they might have done on their own account. We can be reasonably sure of that from the valuable objects, small and easily concealed, which they repacked into the boxes.

The Antechamber finished, the hole in the innermost doorway was refilled, plastered, and stamped with the Royal Necropolis Seal. Then, retracing their steps, the officials closed and sealed the Antechamber door, filled up the plunderers' tunnel through the passage blocking, and made good the outer doorway. What further steps they took to prevent repetition of the crime, we do not know, but probably they buried the whole entrance to the tomb deep out of sight. In the long run nothing but ignorance of its whereabouts could have saved it from further attempts at plundering; and it is certain that between the time of this reclosing and our discovery, no hand had touched the seals upon the door.

CHAPTER NINE

HARD WORK

This chapter is dedicated to those—and they are many —who think that an excavator spends his time basking in the sun, pleasantly exhilarated by watching other people work for him, and otherwise relieved from boredom by having baskets full of beautiful antiquities brought up from the bowels of the earth from time to time for him to look at. His actual life is very different.

Field work is all-important, and if every excavation were properly, systematically, and conscientiously carried out, our knowledge of Egyptian archaeology would be at least 50 per cent greater than it is. There are numberless derelict objects in the storerooms of our museums which would give us valuable information could they but tell us whence they came, box after box full of fragments, which could have been reconstructed if a few notes had been made when they were found. The first and most important rule in excavating is that the archaelogist must remove every antiquity from the ground with his own hands. So much depends upon it. Quite apart from the question of possible damage that might be caused by clumsy fingers, it is essential that he see the object *in situ,* to gain any evidence he can from the position in which it lies, and the relationship it bears to objects near it. For example, there may very likely be dating evidence. How many pieces there are in museums with vague "probably Middle Kingdom" kind of labels which, by reference to the objects with which they were found, might easily have been accurately assigned to the dynasty to which they belonged, or even to the reign of some particular king.

An excavator, then, must see every object in position, must make careful notes before it is moved, and, if necessary, must apply preservative treatment on the spot. Obviously, under these conditions it is all-important for him to keep in close touch with his excavations. Vacations and days off are out of the question. While the work is actually running he must be on the spot all day and available at all hours.

He will not have much time to be idle. To begin with, every tomb, every building, every broken wall even, must be noted.

Then there is photography. Every object of archaeological value must be photographed before it is moved, and in many cases a series of exposures must be made to mark the various stages in the clearing. Many of these photographs will never be used, but the archaeologist can never tell when some question may arise, and a seemingly useless negative become a record of utmost value. Photography is absolutely essential, and it is perhaps the most exacting of all duties the excavator has to face. On a particular piece of work I have taken and developed as many as fifty negatives in a single day.

There are plenty of other jobs to be done, and the excavator's evenings will be very fully occupied if he is to keep up with his work. His notes, his running plans, and the registration of the objects must be kept thoroughly up to date. There are the photographs to be developed, prints to be made, and a register kept of negatives and prints. There will be broken objects to be mended, objects in delicate condition to be treated, restorations to be considered, and beadwork to be rethreaded. Then comes the indoor photography, for each individual object must be photographed to scale, and in some cases from several points of view. The list could be extended almost indefinitely, and would include a number of jobs that would seem to have but a remote connection with archaeology, such as account keeping, looking after workmen, and settling their disputes.

Then, there is the specialist work. Woodwork, for

instance, is seldom in good condition and presents many problems. Damp and the white ant are its chief foes, and in unfavourable conditions nothing will be left of the wood but a heap of black dust or a shell which crumbles at the touch. In the one case, an entry in the notes to the effect that wood has been present is the most that can be done, but in the other there will generally be a certain amount of information to be gleaned.

Preservation of wood, unless in the very last stage of decay, is always possible by application of melted paraffin wax; by this means an object which otherwise would have fallen to pieces can be rendered perfectly solid and fit to handle.

The condition of wood naturally varies according to the site, and, fortunately for us, Luxor was in this respect perhaps the most favourable site in all Egypt. We had trouble with the wood from Tutankhamen's tomb, but it arose, not from the condition in which we originally found it, but from subsequent shrinkage owing to change in atmosphere. This is not such a serious matter in an object of plain wood, but the Egyptians were extremely fond of applying a thin layer of gesso on which they painted scenes or made use of an overlay of gold foil. Naturally, as the wood shrank the gesso covering began to loosen and buckle, and there was considerable danger that large parts of the surface might be lost. The problem is a difficult one. It is a perfectly easy matter to fix paint or gold foil to the gesso, but ordinary preservatives will not fix gesso to wood. Here again we used paraffin wax.

The condition of textiles varies. Cloth in some cases is so strong that it might have come fresh from the loom, whereas in others it has been reduced by damp almost to the consistency of soot. In the present tomb the difficulty of handling it was considerably increased, both by the rough usage to which the garments had been subjected, and by the fact that so many of them were covered with a decoration of gold rosettes and beadwork.

Beadwork is in itself a complicated problem, and will perhaps tax an excavator's patience more than any other material with which he has to deal. The Egyptians were passionately fond of beads, and it is by no means exceptional to find upon a single mummy an equipment consisting of a number of necklaces, two or three collars, a girdle or two, and a full set of bracelets and anklets. In such a case many thousands of beads will have been employed. Very careful work is necessary to secure the original arrangement of beads. The threads which held them together will have rotted away, but nevertheless the beads will be lying in more or less their correct relative positions. Rethreading may be done on the spot, or, better still, the beads may be transferred one by one to a piece of cardboard on which a thin layer of plasticine has been spread. This has the advantage of meaning that one can leave gaps for the missing or doubtfully placed beads.

Papyrus is difficult to handle. If it is in fairly sound condition it can be wrapped in a damp cloth for a few hours, and then it can easily be straightened out under glass. Rolls that are torn and brittle will separate into small pieces during the process of unwrapping, and should never be tackled unless there is plenty of time and space available.

Stone, as a rule, presents few difficulties in the field. In the same way faience, pottery, and metal objects can usually be left for later treatment.

CHAPTER TEN

LABORATORY WORK

Our laboratory was in the long and narrow tomb of Seti II. Here we had established ourselves with our note cards and our preservatives. The objects were brought, still on their stretchers, and covered up until they were wanted. Each in turn was brought up for examination. After the surface dust had been cleared off, measurements, complete archaeological notes, and copies of inscriptions were entered on file cards. Mending and preservative treatment followed, where practicable, after which the object was taken just outside the entrance for scale photographs. Finally it was stored in the innermost recesses of the tomb to wait the final packing.

We had many problems. If we had searched the whole tomb we should have been hard put to find a single object that presented a greater number of them than the wonderful painted casket. Our first care was for the casket itself, which was coated with gesso and covered from top to bottom with brilliantly painted scenes. The surface dust was removed, the discolouration of the painted surfaces was reduced with benzine, and the whole exterior of the casket was sprayed to fix the gesso to the wood, particular attention being paid to tender places at the cracks. Three or four weeks later we noticed that the joint cracks were getting wider, and that the gesso in other places was showing a tendency to buckle. Owing to the change of temperature from the close, humid atmosphere of the tomb to the dry airiness of the laboratory, the wood had begun to shrink once more, and the gesso, not being able to follow it, was coming off from the wood altogether. Drastic measures were necessary, and we decided to use melted paraffin wax. We were thoroughly justified by the result, for the wax penetrated the materials and left everything firm, and, so far from the colours being affected, as we had feared, it seemed to make them more brilliant than before.

It will give some idea of the difficulty of handling this material if I explain that it took me three weeks of hard work to get to the bottom of the box. Immediately after the casket lid was removed and before anything had been touched, we noted that on the right were a pair of rush and papyrus sandals in perfect condition; below them, just showing, a gilt head rest, and, lower again, a confused mass of cloth, leather, and gold. On the left, crumpled into a bundle, was a magnificent royal robe, and in the upper corner there were roughly shaped beads of dark resin. The robe presented us with our first problem, one that constantly recurred—how best to handle cloth that crumpled at the touch, and yet was covered with elaborate and heavy decorations.

This question of cloth and its treatment was enormously complicated by the rough usage to which it had been subjected. Had it been spread out flat or neatly folded, it would have been comparatively simple to deal with. We would have had an easier task if it had been allowed to remain strewn about the floor of the chamber, as the plunderers had left it. Nothing could have been worse than the treatment it had undergone in the tidying-up process, in which the garments had been crushed, bundled, and packed tightly into boxes with a mixture of other most incongruous objects.

In dealing with all these robes there were two alternatives before us. Something had to be sacrificed, and we had to make up our minds whether it should be the cloth or the decoration. It would be quite possible, by the use of preservatives, to secure large pieces of the cloth, but in the process we should inevitably have disarranged and damaged the bead ornamentation that lay below. On the other hand, by sacrificing the cloth, picking it carefully away piece by piece, we could recover, as a rule, the whole scheme of decoration.

Returning to the casket—we began to explore its contents. With very few exceptions—the rush sandals are a case in point—the garments it contained were those of a child. Our first idea was that the king might have kept stored away the clothes he wore as a boy; but later, on one of the belts, and on the sequins of one of the robes, we found the royal cartouche. He must, then, have worn them after he became king, from which it would seem to follow that he was quite a young boy when he succeeded to the throne.

By February, 1923, all the contents of the Antechamber had been transferred to the laboratory, every inch of the floor had been swept and sifted for the last bead or fallen fragment of inlay, and the room stood bare and empty: the stage was ready for the climax of the excavation: we were ready to penetrate the mysteries beyond the sealed door.

CHAPTER ELEVEN

OPENING THE SEALED DOOR

Friday, February 17th, was the day appointed for the great event, and at two o'clock those who were to be privileged to witness the opening ceremony met and filed down the sloping passage into the tomb.

In the Antechamber everything was prepared and ready. We had screened the two sentinel statues with boards to protect them from possible damage, and between them we had erected a small platform, just high enough to enable us to reach the upper part of the doorway, having determined it was safest to work from the top downwards. A short distance back from the platform there was a barrier, and beyond, knowing that there might be hours of work ahead, we had provided chairs for the visitors. On either side of the doorway standards had been set up for our lamps. There before us was the sealed door, and with its opening we were to blot out centuries and stand in the presence of a king who reigned three thousand years ago. My own feelings as I mounted the platform were a strange mixture, and it was with a trembling hand that I struck the first blow.

My first concern was to locate the wooden lintel above the door: then I carefully chipped away the plaster and picked out the small stones which formed the uppermost layer of the filling. The temptation to stop and peer inside at every moment was irresistible. After about ten minutes' work, I had made a hole large enough to insert an electric torch. Its light revealed an astonishing sight. There, within a yard of the doorway, stretching as far as one could see and blocking the entrance to the chamber, stood what looked like a solid wall of gold. For the moment there was no clue as to its meaning, so as quickly as I dared I set to work to widen the hole.

This had now become an operation of considerable difficulty, for the stones of the masonry were not accurately squared blocks built regularly upon one another, but rough slabs of varying size, some to heavy that it took all my strength to lift them. Many of them were left so precariously balanced that the least false movement would have sent them sliding inwards to crash upon the contents of the chamber below. We were also endeavouring to preserve the seal impressions upon the thick mortar of the outer face, and this added considerably to the difficulty of handling the stones.

With the removal of a few stones the mystery of the golden wall was solved. We were at the entrance of the actual burial-chamber of the king, and what barred our way was the side of an immense gilt shrine built to cover and protect the sarcophagus. It took us two hours of hard work to clear away the blocking, and at one point when near the bottom we had to stop for a time to collect the scattered beads from a necklace brought by the plunderers from within the chamber and dropped upon the threshhold. This was a terrible trial to our patience, for it was a slow business, and we were all excited to see what might be within; but finally it was done, the last stones were removed, and the way to the innermost chamber lay open before us.

Fortunately, there were no smaller antiquities at this end of the chamber, so I lowered myself down, and then, taking one of the portable lights, I edged cautiously to the corner of the shrine and looked beyond it. At the corner two beautiful alabaster vases blocked the way, but I could see that if these were removed we should have a clear path to the other end of the chamber. So, carefully marking the spot on which they stood, I picked them up and passed them back to the Antechamber. Lord Carnarvon now joined me, and, picking our way along the narrow passage between shrine and wall, paying out the wire of our light behind us, we investigated further.

Towering above us was one of the great gilt shrines beneath which kings were laid. So enormous was this structure—seventeen by eleven feet, and nine feet high —that it almost filled the entire area of the chamber, a space of only two feet separating it from the walls, while its roof, with cornice top and torus moulding, reached almost to the ceiling. From top to bottom it was overlaid with gold, and upon its sides there were inlaid panels of brilliant blue faience, in which were represented, repeated over and over, the magic symbols which would ensure its strength and safety. On the ground around the shrine were a number of funerary emblems, and, at the north end, the seven magic oars the king would need to ferry himself across the waters of the underworld. The walls of the chamber, unlike those of the Antechamber, were decorated with brightly painted scenes and inscriptions, brilliant in their colours.

Our one thought was of the shrine and its safety. Had the thieves penetrated within it and disturbed the royal burial? Here, on the eastern end, were the great folding doors, closed and bolted, but not sealed, that would answer the question for us. Eagerly we drew the bolts and swung back the doors, and there within was a second shrine with similar bolted doors, and upon the bolts, a seal intact. This seal we determined not to break, for our doubts were resolved, and we could not penetrate farther without risk of serious damage to the monument.

A feeling of intrusion came upon us with the opening of the doors, heightened by the impressiveness of a linen pall, decorated with golden rosettes, which drooped above the inner shrine. We felt that we were in the presence of the dead king and must do him reverence, and in imagination we could see the doors of the successive shrines open one after another till the innermost disclosed the king himself. Carefully and as silently as possible we closed the great swinging doors, and passed on to the farther end of the chamber.

Here a surprise awaited us, for a low door, eastwards from the burial chamber, gave entrance to yet another room, smaller than the outer ones and not so lofty. This doorway, unlike the others, had not been closed and sealed. We were able to see the contents from where we stood, and a single glance told us that here within this little chamber lay the greatest treasures of the tomb. Facing the doorway, on the farther side, stood the most beautiful monument that I have ever seen—so lovely that it made me gasp with wonder and admiration. The central portion was a large shrine-shaped chest, completely overlaid with gold and surmounted by a cornice of sacred cobras. Surrounding this, free standing, were statues of the four tutelary goddesses of the dead, gracious figures with outstretched protective arms, so natural and lifelike in this pose, the expression upon their faces so pitiful and compassionate that one felt it almost sacrilege to look at them. This was undoubtedly the canopic chest containing the jars which play such an important part in the ritual of mummification.

In front of the entrance to the small chamber lay the figure of the jackal god, Anubis, upon his shrine, swathed in linen cloth and resting upon a portable sled. Behind this, the head of a bull upon a stand— emblem of the underworld. On the south side of the chamber lay many black shrines and chests, all closed and sealed except one, whose open doors revealed statues of Tutankhamen standing upon black leopards. On the farther wall were more shrine-shaped boxes and miniature coffins of gilded wood. In the centre of the room there was a row of magnificent caskets of ivory and wood inlaid with gold and blue faience. There were also a number of model boats with sails and rigging all complete, and, at the north side, yet another chariot.

We looked anxiously for evidence of plundering, but on the surface there was none. The thieves must have entered, but they cannot have done more than open two or three of the caskets. Most of the boxes had their seals still intact, and the whole contents of the chamber, in fortunate contrast to those of the Antechamber and the Annexe, remained in position exactly as they had been placed at the time of burial.

How much time we spent on this first survey of the wonders of the tomb I cannot say, but it must have seemed endless to those waiting anxiously in the Antechamber. Not more than three at a time could be admitted with safety. It was curious, as we stood in the Antechamber, to watch their faces, as, one by one, they emerged. Each had a dazed, bewildered look in his eyes, and each in turn as he came out threw up his hands before him, an unconscious gesture of impotence to describe in words the wonders he had seen. It was an experience which no-one could forget, for in imagination—and not wholly in imagination either—we had been present at the funeral ceremonies of a king long dead and almost forgotten.

A week later, the tomb was closed and once again reburied. So ended our preliminary season's work on the tomb of Tutankhamen.

One shadow was to rest upon the work, one regret, which all the world must share—the fact that Lord Carnarvon died in April, 1923, and never saw the fruition of his work. In completion of that work we who carried it out dedicated to his memory the best that lay in us.

CHAPTER TWELVE

THE TOMB AND THE BURIAL CHAMBER

Tutankhamen's tomb is built on much less elaborate
lines than those built in the orthodox Theban manner.
Instead of an elaborate series of corridors, sunken stair-
cases, protective well and vestibule, further descending
passages, antechamber, sepulchral hall, crypt and a
series of four storerooms, his tomb has only a sunken
entrance staircase, a descending passage, an antechamber with an annexe, a burial chamber and one
storeroom. All these rooms are small and of the sim-
plest kind.

The Burial Chamber itself is rectangular; its walls
had been coated with a gypsum plaster and painted
yellow. The rock ceiling was left in its rough and unfinished state. We found traces of smoke, as though
from an oil lamp, on the ceiling in the north-east
corner. The paintings on the walls are all of funereal
and religious subjects. One of the scenes is unprecedented : it shows the figure of Ay, Tutenkhamen's suc-
cessor and the reigning king, presiding over the burial
ceremonies of the boy pharaoh.

Depicted on the east wall is a scene of the funeral
procession : the deceased Tutankhamen, upon a sledge,
is being drawn by courtiers to the tomb. The mummy
is shown supported upon a lion-shaped bier, within a
shrine, on a boat which rests upon the sledge. Over the
dead king are festoons of garlands; on the boat in front
of the shrine is a sphinx rampant; before and behind
the shrine are the mourning goddesses Nephthys and
Isis; and attached to the prow and stern of the boat, as
well as on both sides of the shrine, are red and white
pennants. Courtiers and high officials form the cortège.

On the north wall, east corner, is a scene of historical

Detail from a painted wooden casket

A detail from an ungent vase

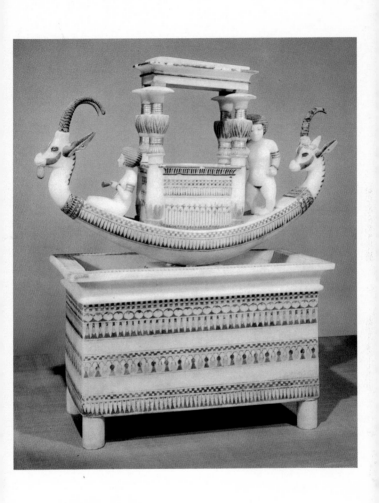

The ornamental Alabaster boat

A pair of Tutankhamen's earrings

importance showing Ay as King, with royal insignia, clad in a leopard's skin of the *Sem* priest. Here King Ay officiates at the funeral ceremony of "The Opening of the Mouth" of the dead Tutankhamen represented as Osiris. Between the living and the dead monarchs are the objects connected with the ceremonial laid out upon a table : the adze, a human finger, the hind limb of an ox, the fan of a single ostrich feather, and a double plume-like object. These are surmounted by a row of five gold and silver cups containing what may be balls of incense such as found in the Antechamber.

When we entered the Burial Chamber we found, lying beside a small hole made by the robbers in the door, portions of two necklaces dropped by a thief. In the south-east corner was a lamp resting upon a trellis-work pedestal, carved out of pure translucent calcite. Its chalicelike cup, which held the oil and a floating wick, was not decorated either on its exterior nor interior surface, yet when the lamp was lit the king and queen were seen in brilliant colours within the thickness of its translucent stone. At first we were puzzled as to how this ingenious effect was achieved. Perhaps the explanation is that there were two cups turned and fitted, one within the other. A picture had been painted in semi-tranparent colours, on the inner cup, and was visible only through the translucent outer cup when the lamp was lit. Beneath this unique lamp, wrapped in reeds, was a silver trumpet, which, though tarnished with age, would still fill the Valley with a resounding blast.

Along the east wall stood Amen's sacred goose of wood, varnished black, and swathed in linen; beside it were two rushwork baskets collapsed with age, and a wine jar bearing the legend : "Year 5, wine of the house of (?) Tutankhamen, from the Western river Chief of the Vintners, Kha."

Resting upon the ground, between the shrine and the north wall of the Burial Chamber, were magic oars to ferry the king's boat across the waters of the Nether

73

World, and with them, one at each end, curious devices in varnished black wood. At the western end of the chamber, were the austere golden emblems of Anubis hung on lotus-shaped poles, standing erect, in alabaster pots placed upon reed mats. They may belong to the dark world under the earth, where the sun sinks, and where, also, the dead sleep : perhaps, emblems to guide the dead through this domain, for was not Anubis— the jackal—a prowler of the dusk, and did not Re send him forth to bury Osiris?

As we drew back the ebony bolts of the great shrine, the doors swung open as if closed only yesterday, and revealed yet another shrine. It had bolted doors, but upon them was a seal intact bearing the name of Tut-ankhamen and a recumbent jackal over Egypt's nine foes. Above the shrine drooped a linen pall. This pall, brown with age, still hanging on its curious wooden supports, was rent by the weight of the gilt bronze daisies sewn to its fabric. The shrine, dazzling from the brilliance of its gold, was decorated in beautiful incised relief with scenes from the book "of that which is in the Underworld"—that guide to the Hereafter, which points out to the dead traveller the road he should take, and explains to him the various evil powers he must meet during his subterranean journey. According to this book two routes, one by water, the other by land, led him to the land of the blessed.

The unbroken seal upon the closed doors of the second strine gave us the data we were seeking. The shrine was intact : the robbers had not reached him. Now, we knew that, within the shrine, we should be treading where no one had entered, and we should be dealing with material untouched and unharmed since the boy king was laid to rest nearly 3,300 years ago. We had at last found what we never dreamed of attaining —an absolute insight into the burial customs of an ancient pharaoh.

In front of the second shrine's doors stood the king and queen's perfume vase, carved of pure alabaster, a rare masterpiece of intricate stone carving embellished with gold and ivory. In front of this beautiful object, partially covered by fallen portions of the pall, stood another powerful piece of conventional art. This was a cosmetic jar of carved calcite, which still held the cosmetic.

On either side, between the two shrines, stacked in the right and left corners, were ceremonial maces, sticks, staffs, and bows, some carefully wrapped in linen. Perhaps the choicest of them all were the gold and silver sticks, made of two thin tubular shafts supporting tiny statuettes of the king, cast and chased in their respective metals. Save for their metals, they are exactly alike and are clearly the products of a master hand. Among other sticks was a plain reed mounted with broad gold and electrum rings and plaited gold wire. We wondered why such an ordinary, plain reed should have been so richly mounted, but the legend written upon it gave the touching solution : "A reed which His Majesty cut with his own hand."

The whole burial chamber and its appointments beautifully represented the mentality of those ancients. Mingled with a fear of the very gods and demons of their own creation one is conscious of sincere feeling and affection for the dead. The meaning of some of the emblems placed in the tomb may have been almost as obscure to the ancient Thebans as to ourselves. The true significance of the symbols might well have been lost years before the age of Tutankhamen and tradition may have held them to be necessary for the welfare of the dead long after the reason for their use had been forgotten.

Besides the traditional paraphernalia necessary to meet and vanquish the dark powers of the Nether World, there were magical figures placed in small recesses in the walls, facing north, south, east, and west, covered with plaster, conforming with the ritual laid down in the Book of the Dead for the defence of the tomb and its owner. Magic, for once, seems to have prevailed. For of twenty-seven monarchs of the imperial age of Egypt buried in this valley, who have suffered every kind of depredation, Tutankhamen alone had lain unscathed throughout thirty-three centuries.

CHAPTER THIRTEEN

CLEARING THE BURIAL CHAMBER AND OPENING THE SARCOPHAGUS

I began the second season's work by removing the two guardian statues that stood before the doorway of the Burial Chamber, and, demolishing the partition wall dividing it from the Antechamber. The demolition of the partition wall gave a clear view of the great outermost shrine, and we were able to see all its grandeur, especially its admirable goldwork and blue faience inlay, overlaid with gilt protective emblems—*Ded*, the amulet of Osiris, and *Thet,* the knot of Isis—alternately.

We worked in a very limited space and a high temperature, and our difficulties were further increased by the great weight of the various sections and panels of which those complex shrines were constructed. These were made of two-and-a-quarter-inch oak planking, overlaid with superbly delicate goldwork upon gesso. The wood planking, though perfectly sound, had shrunk in the course of 3,300 years in that very dry atmosphere, the goldwork upon the gesso had slightly expanded; the result was a space between the basic wood and the ornamental gold surface which, when touched, tended to crush and fall away. We had to deal in that very limited space with those sections of the shrines, weighing from a quarter to three-quarters of a ton, without causing them undue damage.

The outermost shrine, occupying nearly the whole Burial Chamber, measured some seventeen feet in length, eleven feet in width, and over nine feet in height. The four shrines comprised in all some eighty sections, each section or part having to be dealt with differently, and every section first needing to be temporarily treated to allow it to be handled without the least risk of damage.

Then we had to remove and transport to the laboratory all the portable funerary equipment that had been placed around the chamber between the walls and the sides of the outermost shrine, and put up the scaffolding and hoisting tackle preparatory to dismantling the outermost shrine. We began by unhanging the very heavy doors of this shrine. A tedious and hazardous task. Then the panels of the shrine had to be taken off.

The next delicate problem was the linen pall that completely covered the second shrine. Its tissue was much decayed and in a very fragile state; its drooping edges were badly torn from the weight of its own material, and by the metal daisies that were sewn onto it. Happily, duroprene proved most effective in reinforcing the deteriorated fabric. It strengthened the tissues sufficiently to enable us to roll the fabric onto a wooden roller, expressly made for the purpose, and transport it to the laboratory where eventually it would be treated and relined.

The doors of the second shrine were bolted top and bottom, carefully fastened with cord tied to metal staples, and sealed. The clay seal upon this cord was intact. It bore impressions of two distinct seals, one bearing Tutankhamen's personal name, surmounting a jackal over nine foes, the second bore the Royal Necropolis Seal. Behind those two seals we would be dealing with material unharmed since the burial of the king. It was with great care that the cords were severed, those folding doors opened to reveal yet a third shrine, also sealed and intact—the seal impressions upon this third shrine being identical to those on the second shrine.

I carefully cut the cord, removed that precious seal, drew back the bolts, and opened the door. A fourth shrine was revealed, similar in design and even more brilliant in workmanship than the last. The decisive moment was at hand! An indescribable moment for an archaeologist! What was beneath and what did that fourth shrine contain? With intense excitement I drew back the bolts of the last and unsealed doors; they slowly swung open and there, filling the entire area within, stood an immense yellow quartzite sarcophagus intact, with the lid still firmly fixed in its place, just as the pious hands had left it. It was certainly a thrilling moment as we gazed upon the spectacle enhanced by the striking contrast—the glitter of metal—of the golden shrines shielding it. Especially striking were the outstretched hand and wing of a goddess sculptured on the end of the sarcophagus, as if to ward off an intruder. It symbolized an idea beautiful in conception, and, indeed, seemed an eloquent illustration of the perfect faith and tender solicitude for the well-being of their loved ones that animated the people who dwelt in that land over thirty centuries ago.

The three remaining shrines had to be taken to pieces and removed before the problem of the sarcophagus could be contemplated. Thus we laboured for another month, first dismantling the second shrine, then the third, until the fourth was completely freed. When this was achieved we saw that this last shrine had all the appearance of a golden tabernacle. Upon its folding doors and west end were winged figures of the goddesses of the dead, in fine bas-relief, majestic in their protective significance, while the walls of the shrine were covered with religious texts.

We found between the third and fourth innermost shrines ceremonial bows and arrows, and with them, a pair of the gorgeous fans prominent in scenes where kings are depicted. They were beautiful specimens. One, in sheet gold, bore a charming historical scene of the young Tutankhamen in his chariot, followed by his favourite hound, hunting ostriches for feathers for the fan; on the reverse side of the fan, also finely embossed and chased, the young "Lord of Valour" is depicted returning triumphant, his quarry, two ostriches, borne on the shoulders of two attendants who precede him, the plumes under his arm. The second fan, larger and perhaps more resplendent, was of ebony overlaid with sheet gold and encrusted with turquoise, lapis lazuli, and carnelian-coloured glass, as well as translucent calcite : the palm of the fan was emblazoned with the title of Tutankhamen. Only the debris remained of the feathers of these two fans. Although these had suffered from the havoc of insects, enough still remained to show us that there had been alternate white and brown plumes—forty-two on each fan.

The roof and cornice of the fourth innermost shrine, contrary to our expectations, was of different form, and was made in one piece instead of in several sections. It was thus very heavy, and it took several laborious days before it could be lifted, gradually turned, and hauled into the Antechamber. Taking apart the sides, ends, and doors of this innermost shrine was a much easier undertaking. It enclosed and, exactly fitted the sarcophagus. Our task of over eighty days was thus ended.

During the process of our work it became clear that the ancient Egyptian undertakers must have had extreme difficulty in erecting the shrines within that limited space. The carpentry and joining of these constructions exhibited great skill, and each section was carefully numbered and oriented to show not only how they fitted, but also their correct orientation. The constructors of those shrines were past masters in their work, but there was evidence that the obsequies had been hurriedly performed, and that the workmen in charge of those last rites were anything but careful men. They had leaned the parts of the shrines against the four walls around the sarcophagus contrary to instructions, so when the shrines were erected, the doors faced east instead of west, the foot ends west instead of east, and the side panels were likewise transposed. This may have been a pardonable fault, the chamber being so small, but there were other signs of slovenliness. Sections had obviously been banged together, regardless of the risk of damage to their gilt ornamentation. Deep dents from blows from a heavy hammerlike implement were visible on the gold work, in some cases parts of the surfaces had been knocked off, and the workmen's refuse, such as chips of wood, had never been cleared away.

The raising of the roof of the fourth shrine bared the magnificent sarcophagus of wonderful workmanship, carved out of a solid block of finest yellow quartzite, nine feet long, four feet ten inches wide, and four feet ten inches high.

It was on February 3rd that we had our first good look at this sepulchral masterpiece, which ranks amongst the finest specimens in the world. The outstanding features of the sarcophagus are the guardian goddesses Isis, Nephthys, Neith, and Selkit, carved in high relief on each of the four corners, so placed that their full spread wings and outstretched arms encircle the coffin with their protective embrace. Around the base are protective symbols *Ded* and *Thet*. The corners of the casket rested upon alabaster slabs. Between the last shrine and the sarcophagus there were no objects, except for a *Ded*-symbol placed on the south side for strength and possibly protection of the owner.

As our light fell on the great quartzite monument it illuminated, in repeated detail, that last solemn appeal to gods and men, and make us feel that, in the young king's case, a dignity had been added even to death. With the profound silence that reigned, emotion deepened, the past and present seemed to meet—we asked ourselves : was it not yesterday that, with pomp and ceremony, they had laid the young king in that casket? —so fresh, so seemingly recent, were those touching claims on our pity that, the more we gazed on them, the more the illusion gathered strength.

The lid, made of rose granite tinted to match the sarophagus, was cracked in the middle and firmly embedded in the quartzite rim. The cracks had been carefully cemented and painted over to match the rest, in such a way as to leave no doubt that it had not been tampered with. Undoubtedly the original intention must have been made to provide a quartzite lid in keeping with the sarcophagus itself; some accident must have occurred. It may be that the intended lid was not ready in time for the burial of the king, and that this crudely made granite slab was substituted.

The crack greatly complicated the raising of this lid, for had it been intact the operation would have been far easier. However, the difficulty was overcome by passing angle irons along and closely fitting the sides of the slab, which permitted it to be raised by pulleys in one piece.

We had now reached the supreme culminating moment—a moment we had looked forward to for months. All of us were affected by the prospect of what we were about to see—the burial custom of a king of ancient Egypt of thirty-three centuries ago. How would the king be found?

The tackle for raising the lid was in position. I gave the word. Amid intense silence the huge slab, broken in two, weighing over a ton and a quarter, rose from its bed. The light shone into the sarcophagus. A sight met our eyes that at first puzzled and disappointed us. The contents were completely covered by fine linen shrouds. We rolled back these shrouds, one by one, and as the last was removed a gasp of wonderment escaped our lips, so gorgeous was the sight that met our eye: a golden effigy of the young boy king, of most magnificent workmanship, filled the whole of the interior of the sarcophagus. This was the lid of a wonderful coffin in the form of the young king, some seven feet in length, resting upon a low bier in the form of a lion, and no doubt the outermost in a series of coffins, nested one within the other, enclosing the mortal remains of the king. Clasping the body of this magnificent monument were two winged goddesses. Isis and Neith, wrought in rich goldwork upon gesso, as brilliant as the day the coffin was made. While this decoration was rendered in fine bas-relief, the head and hands of the king were in the round, in massive gold of the finest sculpture, surpassing anything we could have imagined. The hands, crossed over the breast, held the royal emblems —the Crook and the Flail—encrusted with deep blue faience. The face and features were wonderfully wrought in sheet gold. The eyes were of aragonite and obsidian, the eyebrows and eyelids inlaid with lapis lazuli. There was a touch of realism, for while the rest of this coffin, covered with feathered ornament, was of brilliant gold, that of the bare face and hands seemed different, the gold of the flesh being of different alloy, thus conveying an impression of the greyness of death. Upon the forehead of this recumbent figure of the king were two emblems delicately worked in brilliant inlay —the Cobra and the Vulture—symbols of Upper and Lower Egypt, but perhaps the most touching, in its human simplicity, was the tiny wreath of flowers around these symbols, as it pleased us to think, the last farewell offering of the widowed girl queen to her husband, the youthful representative of the "Two Kingdoms."

These few withered flowers, still retaining their tinge of colour, told us what a short period 3,300 years really was—but yesterday and tomorrow.

Thus from stairway, steep descending passage, Antechamber and Burial Chamber, from those golden shrines and from that noble sarcophagus, our eyes were now turned to its contents—a gold-encased coffin, in form a recumbent figure of the young king, symbolizing Osiris, or, it would seem, by its fearless gaze, man's ancient trust in immortality. Many disturbing emotions awakened in us, and, in the silence, you could almost hear the ghostly footsteps of the departing mourners.

Our lights were lowered, once more we mounted those sixteen steps, to the light of day, but our inner thoughts still lingered over the splendour of the vanished pharaoh, with his last appeal upon his coffin written upon our minds : "Oh Mother Nut ! spread thy wings over me as the Imperishable Stars."

CHAPTER FOURTEEN

OPENING THE THREE COFFINS

The task before us now was to raise the lid of the first outermost coffin as it rested in the sarcophagus. After careful study of the coffin we decided that the original silver handles—two on each side—were sufficiently well preserved to support the weight of the lid and could be used without danger in raising it. The lid was fixed to the shell by means of ten solid silver tongues, fitted into corresponding sockets in the shell, where they were held in place by substantial gold-headed silver pins. Could we remove the silver pins by which the lid was fixed to the shell of the coffin without disturbing the coffin in the sarcophagus? As the coffin filled up nearly the whole of the interior of the sarcophagus, it was by no means easy to extract the pins. By careful manipulation, however, it was found possible to withdraw them, except for the pin at the head end where there was only space enough to pull it half out. It had to be filed through before the inner half could be withdrawn.

The next step was to place in position the hoisting tackle necessary for lifting the lid. The tackle was attached to the handles of the lid of the coffin by means of slings, thus assuring a correct centralization of its weight, otherwise there would have been a danger of the lid bumping against the sides of the sarcophagus.

It was a moment as anxious as exciting. The lid came up fairly readily, revealing a second magnificent coffin, covered with a thin gossamer linen sheet, darkened and much decayed. Lying on this linen shroud were floral garlands, composed of olive and willow leaves, petals of the blue lotos, and cornflowers, while a small wreath of similar kind had been placed, also over the shroud, on the emblems of the forehead. Underneath this covering were rich multicoloured glass decorations encrusted upon the fine goldwork of the coffin.

So far our progress had been fairly satisfactory, but we now became conscious of a rather ominous feature. The second coffin showed distinct signs of the effect of some form of dampness and, here and there, tendency for its beautiful inlay to fall away. This was disconcerting, suggesting as it did the existence of former humidity of some kind within the nest of coffins. Should this prove the case, the preservation of the royal mummy would be less satisfactory than we had hoped.

We had to consider how to deal with the second coffin, as well as the shell of the first. Our difficulties were increased on account of the depth of the sarcophagus, and it was evident that the outer shell and the second coffin, neither of which was in a condition to bear much handling, must be raised together. This we eventually accomplished by means of pulleys attached by steel pins passed through the tongue sockets of the first outermost shell, and in spite of their great weight the coffins were successfully raised to just above the top of the sarcophagus, and wooden planks were passed under them.

I took more notes, and then was able to remove the chaplet and garlands, and roll back the covering shroud. We could now gaze with admiring eyes upon the finest example of the ancient coffin-maker's art ever yet seen, most delicate in conception, and very beautiful in line. As it lay in the outer shell resting upon the improvised trestles, it presented a wonderful picture of Majesty lying in State.

This second coffin, six feet eight inches long, sumptuously inlaid on thick gold foil with cut, and engraved opaque glass, simulating red jasper, lapis lazuli, and turquoise, was similar in form and design to the first. It symbolizes Osiris, but it differs in certain detail. In this case the king wears the *Nemes* head-dress and the body is embraced by the vulture, Nekhebet, and the serpent, Buto. Its most arresting feature is the delicacy and superiority of the conception, which make it a masterpiece.

We were now faced by a complicated problem. Since there were handles on the outer coffin for lowering or raising the lid, we expected similar metal handles on the second coffin. There were none, and their absence placed us in a dilemma. The second coffin proved exceedingly heavy; its decorated surface very fragile. It fitted the outer shell so closely that it was not possible to pass one's little finger between the two. Its lid was fixed, as in the case of the outer coffin, with gold-headed silver pins which, as the coffin lay in the outer shell, could not be extracted. It would have to be lifted in its entirety from the outer shell before anything further could be done.

We could not be sure that the wood of the coffin was sufficiently well preserved to bear its own weight. However, after long consultations and having studied the problem for nearly two days, we devised a plan. To remove the second coffin from the shell of the first, some points of attachment were necessary. We decided to make use of the metal pins which fastened down the lid. Inspection showed that although the space between the shell of the outer coffin and the second coffin was insufficient to enable us to withdraw these pins entirely, they could still be pulled out about a quarter of an inch, so as to permit stout copper wire attachments to be fixed to them and to the overhead scaffold. This we did successfully. Strong metal eyelets were then screwed into the top edge of the shell of the outer coffin, so that it could be lowered from the second coffin by means of ropes working on the pulleys.

On the following day we were able to proceed with the next stage. It proved to be one of the most important moments in the dismantling of the tomb. The process adopted was the reverse of that which might appear to be natural. We lowered the outer shell from the second coffin, instead of lifting the second coffin out of the first, because the headroom was insufficient, and the weight being stationary, there would be less risk of stress on those ancient silver pins. The shell of the outer coffin was lowered once again into the sarcophagus, leaving, for a moment, the second coffin suspended in midair by means of the ten stout wire attachments. A wooden tray sufficiently large to span the opening of the sarcophagus was then passed under it, and the second coffin, strongly supported, stood before us free and accessible. The wire attachments were severed and the overhead gear removed, Mr Burton took his photographs, and we were able to turn our energies to raising its lid.

The entire inlaid surface was indeed in a very fragile condition, and any handling had to be avoided. In order to lift the lid without causing injury, metal eyelets, to serve as handles, were screwed into it at four points where there would be no danger of permanent disfigurement. To these eyelets our hoisting tackle was fixed, the gold-headed silver nails were extracted, and the lid was slowly raised. There was some tendency for the lid to stick, but gradually it rose from its bed and, when high enough to clear the contents of the coffin, it was lowered onto a wooden tray.

This revealed a third coffin, also, Osiride in form, but the main details of the workmanship were hidden by a close-fitting reddish-coloured linen shroud. The burnished gold face was bare; placed over the neck and breast was an elaborate bead and floral collarette, sewn upon a backing of papyrus, and tucked immediately above the Nemes head-dress was a linen napkin. I then removed the floral collarette and linen coverings —and an astounding fact was disclosed : this third coffin, six feet, one-and-three-quarter inches long, was solid gold ! The mystery of the enormous weight, as much as eight strong men could lift, which puzzled us, was now clear.

The face of this gold coffin was again that of the king, but the features though conventional, by symbolising

Osiris, were even more youthful than those on the other coffins. In actual design it reverted to that of the outermost coffin and had engraved upon it figures of Isis and Nephthys, but auxiliary to this design were winged figures of Nekhebet and Buto. These later protective figures, emblematic of Upper and Lower Egypt, were the prominent feature, for they were superimposed in gorgeous and massive cloisonné work over the richly engraved ornament of the coffin—their inlay being natural semi-precious stones. In addition to this decoration, over the conventional collarette of "the Hawk"— again in cloisonné work—was a double detachable necklace of large disk-shaped beads of red and yellow gold and blue faience, which enhanced the richness of the whole effect. But the ultimate details of the ornamentation were hidden by a black lustrous coating due to liquid unguents that had evidently been profusely poured over the coffin. As a result this unparalleled monument was not only disfigured—only temporarily, as it afterward proved—but was stuck fast to the interior of the second coffin, the consolidated liquid filling up the space between the second and third coffins almost to the level of the lid of the third.

These consecration unguents, which had obviously been used in great quantity, were doubtless the cause of the disintegration observed when dealing with the outer coffins which, as they were in a practically hermetically sealed quartzite sarcophagus, cannot have been affected by outside influences. The covering shroud and floral collarette mingled with blue faience beads had also suffered, and although these at first appeared to be in good condition, they proved so brittle that the material broke the instant it was touched.

We raised the third coffin contained in the shell of the second, which now rested on the top of the sarcophagus, and moved them into the Antechamber where they were more accessible for examination and manipulation. It was then that the wonder and magnitude of our last discovery more completely dawned upon us.

This unique and wonderful monument—a coffin over six feet in length, of the finest art, wrought in solid gold about one-tenth of an inch thick—represented an enormous mass of pure bullion.

How great must have been the wealth buried with those ancient pharaohs! What riches that valley must have once concealed! Of the twenty-seven monarchs buried there, Tutankhamen was probably of the least importance. The plundering of royal tombs becomes easily intelligible when the incentive to these crimes is measured by this gold coffin.

Our object now was to protect from injury and to conserve the delicate inlay on the shell of the second coffin. Therefore it was lightly brushed to remove loose dust, sponged with warm water and ammonia, and, when dry, the whole surface covered with a thick coating of paraffin wax applied hot with a long brush. This wax was as it cooled and solidified held the inlay securely in position so that the coffin could be handled easily.

Then we had to experiment to find the most satisfactory and the quickest manner of dealing with those ancient consecration unguents that not only covered the body of the coffin but completely filled the space between the two, thus sticking them fast and for the moment preventing further progress. This substance was black and resembled pitch; where the layer was thin it was hard and brittle, but where a thicker layer had accumulated, the interior of the material was soft and plastic. When warm it smelled somewhat fragrant, not unpleasant, and suggestive of wood pitch.

It follows that this substance could be melted by heat and dissolved by certain solvents, but neither of these methods was practicable. So we decided to raise the lid of the third coffin and examine the contents before applying any drastic measures. Luckily the line of junction between the lid and the coffin was visible and, with difficulty, assessible, except at the extreme foot end where the second and third coffins practically touched.

The lid was fastened to the shell by means of eight tenons (four on each side), which were held in their sockets by nails. Thus if the nails could be extracted the lid could be raised. In the narrow space between the two coffins ordinary implements for extracting metal pins were useless, and others, had to be devised. With long screwdrivers converted to meet the conditions, the solid gold nails were removed piecemeal. The lid was raised by its golden handles and the mummy of the king disclosed.

Three thousand years and more had elapsed since men's eyes had gazed into that golden coffin. Here at last lay all that was left of the youthful pharaoh, hitherto little more to us than the shadow of a name.

Before us, occupying the entire interior of the golden coffin was an impressive, neat, and carefully made mummy, over which had been poured anointing unguents, as in the case of the outside of its coffin, again in great quantity, consolidated and blackened by age. In contrast to the general dark and sombre effect, due to these unguents, was a brilliant, magnificent, burnished gold mask of the king, which covered his head and shoulders, which, like the feet, had been intentionally avoided when using the unguents. The mummy was fashioned to symbolise Osiris. The beaten gold mask, a beautiful and unique specimen of ancient portraiture, bears a sad but calm expression suggestive of youth overtaken prematurely by death. Upon its forehead, wrought in massive gold, were the royal insignia—the Nekhebet Vulture and Buto Serpent, emblems of the Two Kingdoms over which he had reigned. To the chin was attached the conventional Osiride beard, wrought in gold and lapis-lazuli-coloured glass; around the throat was a triple necklace of yellow and red gold and blue faience disk-shaped beads; pendant from the neck by flexible gild inlaid straps was a large black resin scarab that rested between the hands. The burnished gold hands, crossed over the breast, separate from the mask, were sewn to the material of the linen wrappings, and grasped the Flagellum and Crozier—the emblems of Osiris. Immediately below these was the simple outermost linen covering, adorned with richly inlaid gold trappings pendant from a large figure of the *Ba* bird or soul, of gold cloisonné work, its full-spread wings stretched over the body. The consecration unguents disguised their detail and brilliance, and in many objects they had caused disastrous deterioration. When these trappings were cleaned it became clear that the jeweller had made the main parts to measure, but the finished mummy proved larger than was originally expected, and that pieces were cut, others added, to make them fit.

Though the attributes of the mummy are those of the gods, the features are certainly those of Tutankhamen, comely and placid. From certain aspects the face resembles that of his father-in-law Akhenaten, but in profile it shows an even stronger likeness to the great Queen Tyi, Akhenaten's mother. When the detailed photographs had been taken, we were better able to examine the actual state of preservation of the mummy. The greater part of the flagellum and crozier was completely decomposed, and had already fallen to dust; the threads that once held the hands and trappings in place upon the outer linen covering were decayed, and in consequence the various sections fell apart at the slightest touch; the black resin scarab was covered by minute fissures, probably the result of contraction; consequently these external trappings and ornaments had to be removed, piece by piece, and placed in corresponding order and position upon a tray for future cleaning and remounting. The further we got the more evident it became that the coverings and the mummy were both in a perilous state. They were completely carbonised by the reactions set up by the fatty acids of the unguents with which they had been saturated. But even worse, both the mask and the mummy were stuck fast to the bottom of the coffin by the consolidated residue of the unguents, and no amount of legitimate force could move them. What was to be done?

We knew that this adhesive material could be softened by heat, and we hoped that an exposure to the midday sun would melt it sufficiently to allow the mummy to be lifted. A trial was made for several hours in sun temperature reaching as high as 149°, without any success and, as other means we not practicable, it meant that we should have to make all further examination of the king's remains as they lay in the two coffins.

After the scientific examination of the king's mummy *in situ,* and its final removal from the gold coffin, the very difficult question of removing the gold mask and extricating the gold coffin from the shell of the second coffin had to be solved.

Originally something like two bucketfuls of the liquid unguents had been poured over the golden coffin, and a similar amount over the body inside. As heat was the only feasible method of melting the unguent, in order to apply a temperature sufficiently high for the purpose, without causing damage, the interior of the golden coffin had to be completely lined with thick plates of zinc which would not melt under a temperature of 968°. The coffins were then placed upside down on trestles, the outside one being protected against heat and fire by blankets saturated and kept wet with water. Our next step was to place several paraffin lamps burning at full blast under the hollow of the gold coffin. The heat from the lamps had to be regulated to keep the temperature well within the melting point of zinc. In fact the coating of wax upon the surface of the second coffin acted as a pyrometer—while it remained unmelted under the wet blanketing there was no fear of injury.

Although the temperature was 932°, it took several hours before any real effect was noticeable. At the first sign of movement the lamps were turned out, and the coffins left suspended upon the trestles, where after an

The Canopic Equipment

The third coffin

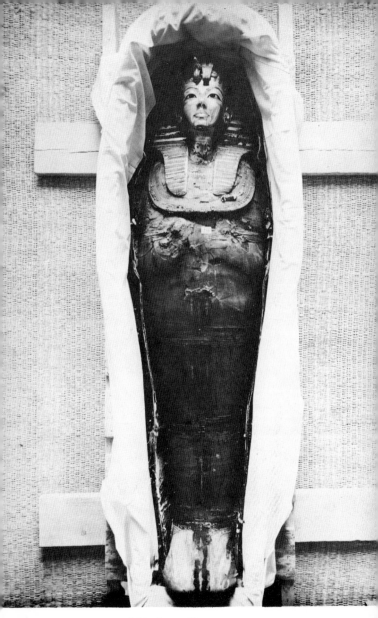

The royal mummy within its coffin

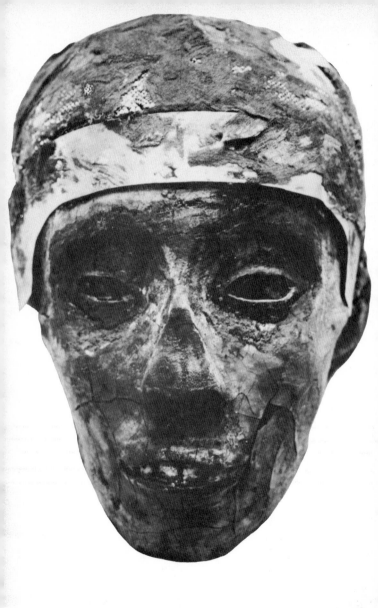

The head of the king's mummy as first revealed

The king on the back of a leopard

The interior of box 54 showing the scattered parts of the corslet

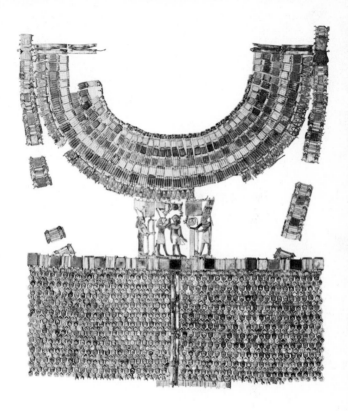

. . . and the corslet after reconstruction

The top of a gold stick showing the king aged about twelve

hour, they began to fall apart. We were able to separate them by lifting up the second coffin, and leaving the shell of the gold coffin resting upon the trestles. It was hardly recognisable: all we could see was a dripping mass of viscous pitchlike material which proved very difficult to remove.

The inside was also covered with a glutinous mess, to which the gold mask still stuck. This mask had been protected by being bound with a folded wet blanket continually fed with water, its face padded with wet wadding. As it had been subjected to the full power of the heat collected in the interior of the coffin, it was freed and lifted away quite easily, although a great mass of sticky unguents adhered to its back, which we removed with the aid of a blast lamp and solvents.

The first coffin had to be raised out of the sarcophagus. We did this by hoisting tackle attached to the overhead scaffolding. When it cleared the top of the sarcophagus, a wooden tray was passed beneath it, and it was thus carried up to the laboratory, where its lid was already under treatment. It was very heavy, and, like the shrines, was probably of oak.

Now, the only remaining object in the sarcophagus was the gilt bed-shaped bier with lion's head and feet. It stood on the bottom and served as a support to the first (outermost) coffin. It was made of a stout and heavy wood covered with gesso-gilt; but the astonishing fact was that after supporting the weight—more than a ton and a quarter—of those three great coffins for over thirty centuries, it was still intact. Strips of broad webbing were passed under it, and this splendid example of ancient Egyptian construction was lifted out of the sarcophagus. It stood about twelve inches high, seven feet six inches long, and was curved so as to fit the base of the outermost coffin. The central panel was designed in low relief to represent a cord-mesh. The joints of the framework were hardly sprung, thus bearing witness to the good quality of the wood and the extreme excellence of the joinery.

The Burial Chamber and sarcophagus were now empty and we were able, for the first time, to reconsider what we had learnt from this tomb of the burial of a pharaoh.

The more we considered it the more we were impressed by the care and enormous costliness lavished by the Egyptians on the enshrinement of their dead. Barrier after barrier was raised to guard their remains from the predatory hands against which, in death, these great kings so ineffectually sought protection. The process was as elaborate as it was costly, and the modern observer cannot help but be astounded at the enormous labour and expense lavished on these royal burials, even when the titanic excavations of their rock-cut tombs is disregarded. Undoubtedly the greatest ceremony which awaited every Egyptian pharaoh was his funeral : all pharaohs made elaborate arrangements for their own burial places for they believed that they were constructing not merely their tomb, but their heaven also.

CHAPTER FIFTEEN

THE EXAMINATION OF THE ROYAL MUMMY

On November 11, 1925, at 9.45 a.m., the examination of the royal mummy commenced, and now our work became of transcending interest.

The external ornaments and inlaid gold trappings had been removed, the king's mummy lay bare with its simple outer coverings and gold mask. It occupied the whole of the interior of the gold coffin, measuring in total length six feet, one inch.

Because of the fragile and carbonised condition of the linen swathing, the exposed surface was painted over with melted paraffin wax. When it congealed, it formed a thin coating on the surface, with minimum penetration of the decayed wrappings beneath. When the wax had cooled, Dr. Douglas Derry made a longitudinal incision down the centre of the outer binding to the depth penetrated by the wax, enabling the consolidated layer to be removed in large pieces. But the voluminous underwrappings were found to be in even worse condition of carbonisation and decay. We had hoped, by removing a thin outer layer of bandage from the mummy, to free it so that it might be removed, but we were again disappointed. It was found that the linen beneath the mummy and the body itself were so saturated in the annointing oils which formed a pitchlike mass at the bottom of the coffin and held it embedded so firmly, that it was impossible to raise it except at the risk of great damage. Even after most of the bandages had been carefully removed, the solidified matter had to be chiselled away from beneath the limbs and trunk before it was possible to raise the king's remains.

The bandages that actually enveloped the head were

in a better state of preservation than those on the body.

The general system of bandaging seemed to be the usual one : it comprised a series of bandages, sheets, and pads of linen, (where the latter were required to complete the human form), the whole showing evidence of considerable care. The linen was very fine. The numerous objects found upon the mummy were caught up in many different layers of bindings which were wound crosswise and transversely.

The removal of the final wrappings that protected the face of the king needed the utmost care, as there was always the risk of injury to the fragile features. At the touch of a sable brush the last few fragments of decayed fabric fell away, revealing a serene and placid countenance, that of a young man. The face was refined and cultured, the features well formed, especially the clearly marked lips, and the first and most striking impression of all present was the remarkable structural resemblance to his father-in-law, Akhenaten.

There is one more point of great interest. The king's head shows that the finer contemporary representations of him upon the monuments beyond all doubt, are accurate portraits of Tutankhamen.

Upon the king's neck there are two kinds of symbolical collars and twenty amulets grouped in six layers; and between each of these layers were numerous linen bandages.

This profusion of amulets and sacred symbols placed on the neck of the king are extremely significant, suggesting as they do how greatly the dangers of the underworld were feared for the dead. No doubt they were intended to protect him against injury on his journey through the hereafter. The quality and quantity of these protective symbols would naturally depend on his high rank and wealth, as well as upon the affection of his survivors. The actual meaning of many of them is not clear, nor do we know the powers ascribed to them. However, we do know that they were placed there for the help and guidance of the dead, and made as beautiful and as costly as possible.

In accordance with the Book of the Dead, whoever wears the *Ded*—the emblem of Osiris—may "enter into the realms of the dead, eat the food of Osiris, and be justified." He on whom the *Thet* symbol—the girdle of Isis—is hung, will be guarded by Isis and Horus, and be welcomed with joy into the Kingdom of Osiris.

We learn also from the Book of the Dead that when these mystic emblems were placed on the deceased, the magic spells associated with them were to be uttered "in solemn voice." In the case of the amulets and symbols found upon the king, there were traces of a small papyrus that bore a ritual, written in white linear hieroglyphs, but too decayed and disintegrated to allow practical conservation, though here and there names of gods, such as Osiris and Isis, were with difficulty decipherable. This diminutive document, disintegrated beyond recovery, possibly pertained to such spells.

Although we examined the mummy itself with as much precision as was possible in its charred state, we could find no traces of the cause or causes of the young king's death, but the masses of swathings, ornaments and amulets at least conveyed to us that great care had been taken with his mortal remains in preparation for his future life.

CHAPTER SIXTEEN

A TREASURY BEYOND THE
BURIAL CHAMBER

We next directed our energies towards the Store-room beyond the Burial Chamber, perhaps better named "The Innermost Treasury."

This room is not more than fifteen feet eight inches long, by twelve feet six inches wide and seven feet eight inches in height. We entered by a low open doorway cut in the northern end of the west wall of the Burial Chamber. It is of extreme simplicity, there being no attempt at decoration. In fact, it is just as those ancient Egyptian masons left it—even the last few flakes of limestone from their chisels lay on the floor.

Small and simple as it is, the impressive memories of the past haunt it none the less. But however much one may respect the past, an archaeologist's duty is to the present. It is for him to interpret what is hidden.

The doorway of this little room was guarded by the jackal-like dog Anubis, covered with linen and couchant upon a gilt pylon. But unquestionably thieves had entered, although they seem to have done little harm other than to open and rifle the treasure caskets and some boxes. At first sight, the only visible evidence of their visit were some beads and tiny fragments of jewellery scattered on the floor, the broken seals and displaced lids of caskets, folds of linen hanging from the mouth of the boxes, and here and there an overturned object. The robbers must have been aware of the purely mystic nature of the contents of this room for, with rare exception, only those boxes which held objects of intrinsic value had been disturbed.

Among a varied collection we found the canopic equipment, safeguards for the deceased's passage through the Underworld; objects that the deceased required for his use in daily life, and would continue to require in his future life: jewellery for his adornment, chariots for his recreation, and servants (*Shawabti*-figures) to carry out any irksome work he might be called upon to do in the hereafter. Housed in black shrinelike chests were statuettes representing the king in the act of divine pursuit and figures of the gods, to help him through the dangers to which he might be exposed. There were also barques, fully rigged and equipped with cabins, symbolising the funeral pilgrimage; there was a granary filled with grain; a saddlestone for grinding corn; strainers for the preparation of beer; and there was even a mock figure representing the resurrection of Osiris, the god of the dead, who, like man, suffered death, was buried, and afterward rose again to immortal life.

It was a firm conviction among the ancient Egyptians that life did not end at death, but that man continued to live just as he had lived upon this earth, provided that measures for his protection to usher him through the labyrinth of the underworld and necessities for his future existence were assured him.

The figure of the god Anubis, who takes upon himself the form of a kind of black jackal-like dog without gender, who not only presided over the burial rites but also acted as the vigilant watcher over the dead, was appropriately placed in the open doorway, facing outward towards the west. It enabled him to watch over the Burial Chamber and its occupant while he also guarded his domain the "Treasure of the Innermost."

The magical torch and clay-brick pedestal found at the entrance of this room, with its tiny reed torch and a few grains of charcoal, seem not to have been dropped by mere chance on the floor within the threshold in front of Anubis. The magical formula scratched upon the brick tells us: "It is I who hinder the sand from choking the secret chamber. I am for the protection of Osiris (the deceased)."

To depart for a moment from the main subject; what was the origin of this very interesting Anubis animal? The majority of the animal's characteristics are those of the domestic dog, but in place of the curved tail peculiar to the dog, it has the long, straight tail of the fox, club-like in form, which it carried in drooping position like the wolf, jackal, or fox. The numerous representations of this Anubis animal upon the Egyptian monuments resemble largely the bearing of the jackal, and it may have been a domesticated form of the jackal crossed with another breed of dog. The collar and the scarflike leash that are invariably represented round its neck also suggest an animal brought under human control. And when one takes into account the qualities of the domesticated dog—devotion to his master, knowledge and defence of his property, attachment to him until death—it may explain why the Egyptians chose this jackal-like dog as the vigilant watcher over their dead.

The fact that this animal is invariably represented genderless suggests the possibility of its being an imaginary beast.

The canopic equipment stood before the centre of the east end wall immediately opposite the entrance doorway. It was six feet six inches in height, and it occupied a floor area of some five by four feet. The monument's simple grandeur, and the calm which seemed to accompany the four little gracious statuettes that guarded it, produced a mystery and an appeal to the imagination that would be difficult to describe.

The shielding canopy overlaid with gold was supported by four corner posts upon a massive sledge, its cornice surmounted with brilliantly inlaid solar cobras; on each side was a lifelike gilded statutette of a tutelary goddess, guarding her charge with outstretched protective arms. The central portion—a large shrine-shaped chest—also completely overlaid with gold and surmounted with solar cobras, concealed a smaller chest hewn out of a solid block of veined semitranslucent alabaster (calcite). This alabaster chest, with gilt dado, covered with a linen pall, standing upon a silver-handled gesso-gilt wooden sledge, held the four receptacles for the internal organs of the king. The organs, wrapped in separate packages in the shape of a mummy were in four miniature gold coffins.

In the Egyptian process of mummifying the body, the internal organs were separately preserved in four receptacles and charged to the genii Imsety, Hepy, Duamutef, and Qebehsnewef, who were under the special protection of the goddesses Isis, Nepthys, Neith, and Selkit. Each of these four tutelary goddesses was supposed to have possessed within herself a genius, which it was her duty to protect. An ancient myth connected with the four genii, said to be the sons of Horus, tells us that they arose from water in a lily, and that the crocodile god, Sebekh, commanded by the sun god, Re, had to catch them in a net. However, it is also said that Isis produced them, and that they succoured Osiris in his misfortunes, and saved him from hunger and thirst, and hence it became their office to do the same for the dead.

After the mummy, its coffins, sarcophagus, and covering shrines, the most important among the funeral appurtenances was the canopic equipment for the viscera. The canopic chest had on its four corners the four guardian goddesses carved in high relief—Isis on the southwest corner, Nephthys on the northwest corner, Neith on the southeast, and Selkit on the northeast. The interior of the chest was carved out only five inches deep, but sufficiently to give the appearance of four rectangular compartments each containing a jar. Covering the tops of each of the imitation jars were separate human-headed lids, finely sculptured in alabaster in the likeness of the king. The two jars on the east side faced west, and the two on the west side faced east. In each hollow, wrapped in linen, was an exquisite miniature gold coffin which held the viscera, elaborately inlaid and resembling the second coffin of the king. The coffins were placed upright, facing in the same direction as the alabaster lids. These miniature coffins are wonderful specimens of both goldsmith's and jeweller's art.

But in spite of all this care and costly expenditure to preserve and protect the mortal remains of the young king, the sumptuous funerary equipment, and what must have been elaborate funerary rites at the time of entombment, we find gross carelessness on the part of those people who undertook the burial rites.

The ancient Egyptians must have known better than we do now that the goddess Nephthys should be on the south side of the chest, and that her charge was the genius Hepy and that Selkit should be on the east side, and her charge was the genius Qebehsnewef. Yet in erecting this canopic equipment, even though it bears distinct marks as well as distinguishing inscriptions upon each side, they place Selkit south in the place of Nephthys, and Nephthys east where Selkit should have been. Moreover, the carpenters who put together the sections of the canopy and fitted the wooden covering over the alabaster chest left their refuse (wood chips) in a heap on the floor of the chamber.

There was a flotilla of model craft. These models were made of logs of wood, pinned together, shaped and planed with the adze. They are painted and gilded and in some instances highly decorated with brilliant ornamentation. Two had been overturned by the thieves. The remainder of the craft were discovered in the Annexe—unfortunately these were almost entirely broken up by plunderers. Among these boats were ships to follow the voyage of the sun; canoes for hunting the hippopotamus and fowling in the hereafter, symbolising the mythical pastimes of Horus in the marshes; vessels for the holy pilgrimage to and from Abydos; and craft to render the deceased independent of the favours of the "celestial ferrymen" to reach the "fields of the blessed," that are surrounded by seething waters difficult to traverse.

On the north side of the room was a row of treasure caskets and plain white boxes which had been attacked by the tomb plunderers for the gold and silver articles that they contained. Their seals were broken, their contents ransacked, their pieces of greater value stolen.

At least 60 percent of the original contents was missing from these boxes. What was left of the jewellery comprises: some ear-rings, a necklace, a number of pectoral ornaments, some bracelets and a ring. There were also a lid of a small openwork jewelled box, some sceptres, two mirror cases, the residue of some vestments, and a writing outfit—forty-three pieces in all. The exact amount of jewellery stolen is impossible to estimate, but we can tell that two mirrors and at least twenty vessels from two of the caskets, four of which are stated to have been of gold, were stolen.

The "sergeants of the necropolis," who resealed the tomb after the raid, seem to have carried out their duty in a careless and perfunctory manner. What was left had evidently been gathered up and put back into the caskets regardless of the original order. We found parts of one ornament in one casket, parts in another, and the whole mass in confusion.

There was more than enough to enable us to study the skill of the jeweller, as well as the goldsmith's work in the royal workshops of the late Eighteenth Dynasty. The metals employed were gold, electrum, silver and, in a lesser degree, bronze; the natural stones were amethyst, turquoise, lapis lazuli, calcite, carnelian, chalcedony, green felspar, semitranslucent and translucent quartz (often backed with pigment for brilliance and imitative effects), serpentine, and an obscure hard olive-green stone not identified. In addition to these were composite materials such as faience (glazed pottery), hard vitreous paste, and semi-translucent and opaque coloured glasses, used in the place of stones. But perhaps the most remarkable material used in the composition of this jewellery was a dark coloured resin, both on ornaments and as beads. Another peculiarity in these ornaments is a brilliant scarlet-tinted gold. This, when overlaid with bright yellow gold ornamentation, such as the granulated goldwork, and in combination with the dark coloured resin, gives a strange and somewhat barbaric effect.

The theme employed in these ornaments has a strong connection with the state religion. Of these designs Re, the sun god, and Aah, the Moon god, are the nucleus, if not the principal. With the ancient Egyptians, especially at this moment, there was no god of higher standing than Re. They regarded him as the Master of the Universe, who, from his sacred barque in the heavens, governed all things. To speak of God was to think of Re. Re, the sun itself, "Lord of Heaven." "The Sovereign King of all Life," takes many forms in this jewellery, such as Khepre, Horus, Harakhte, and Atum, each being a local representative of some phase of the sun. Khepre, the scarab, is a transformation of the sun god in the form of the famous dung-beetle. It was in this form that the newly born sun issues from the "Cavern of Dawn" to begin his diurnal career. On his awakening in the East he enters into the morning barque to ascend the heavenly vault, when he is identified with Horus, either as a youth or as a Hobby falcon. A prayer refers to Re with these words : "Beautiful is Thine awakening, O Horus, who voyagest over the sky. . . . The fire-child with glittering rays, dispelling darkness and gloom." As he triumphantly hovers in mid-air, he is conceived as a great disk with multicoloured wings ready to pounce upon his foe. During his heavenly course he also takes the shape of Harakhte, either as a falcon-headed man, or as a peregrine falcon, a highly courageous bird of prey that kills its quarry upon the wing. Finally he becomes the old man, Atum, "the Closer of the Day," enters into the evening barque, and descends behind Manun, the sacred Mountain of the West, into the underworld to begin again his nocturnal journey through the twelve caverns—the hours of the night. There, he give light to the great god Osiris, "the Ruler of Eternity."

From such mythological considerations as these,

there can be little doubt that Pharaonic jewellery was looked upon as sacred. The Egyptians may have believed it to possess magic powers; it may be, too, that priestly orders attached to the court had special charge of it. Underlying the design there certainly appears to lurk an ulterior idea. Thus we find these jewels of Tutankhamen, though perhaps made for daily use, designed so as to serve a purpose in the world to come.

We found ear-rings among this jewellery which seem to have belonged to Tutankhamen in his earlier youth because when we examined the mummy of Tutenkhamen, we found that his ear lobes were pierced, but among the numerous ornaments that we discovered within his wrappings there was nothing of the nature of an ear-ring. The gold portrait mask that covered his head also had pierced ear lobes, but the holes had been carefully filled in with small disks of thin sheet gold, suggesting an endeavour to hide the fact. Among the representations of kings upon monuments, pierced ear lobes are often marked, but I am not aware of any instance of actual ear-rings being depicted on a king's ears.

Perhaps the most important objects among this collection of jewellery are the insignia of royalty : the two crozier sceptres and two flagella. The crozier, or kind of pastoral staff, was one of the insignia of Osiris. It was held in the left hand of both the god and the king. It takes the form of a short staff ending at the top in a crook bent inward and outward. In this case it is made up of sections of gold, dark blue glass, and obsidian, upon a bronze core.

The flagellum, a kind of whip or scourge commonly known as the "flail," was the complement to the crozier sceptre and the second of the insignia proper of Osiris. It was held by both the god and the king in the right hand. It consists of a short handle, bent at an acute angle at the top, to which are attached three "swingles" by means of beaded thongs, in such a manner as to enable them to swing freely. The larger flagellum bears the prenomen and nomen of Tutankhamen; the smaller one bears his Aten name in place of the Amen name, suggesting that it belonged to the earlier part of the young king's reign before he was converted to the worship of Amen. Its smaller size is also in keeping with this hypothesis. It becomes evident that these insignia were symbols of authority over the two principal factions in early times; the husbandmen and the shepherds.

The numerous sepulchral statuettes called *Shawabti*-figures, representing the king swathed in linen, are mummiform. Such figures were originally made of *Shawabti* wood whence they derive their name; and their function, according to the sixth chapter of the Book of the Dead, was to act as substitute for the deceased in the netherworld, if he be called upon to perform any fatiguing duties.

Their implements—the hoe, the pick, the yoke, basket, and water vessel—either depicted upon the figures or placed with them as copper and faience models, clearly indicate the duty which they were supposed to perform for their deceased lord in the future life.

Related to the *Shawabti*-figures and reminiscent of Osiris we also found in this room a kind of miniature effigy of the dead king in a small oblong chest, carefully padded with linen. This effigy was made by Maya, the Overseer of the Works in the Place of Eternity (that is, the tomb). Maya was in all probability responsible for the excavation of the king's tomb, and it is possible that he was also responsible for the resealing of Tutankhamen's tomb.

Placed on the top of the kiosks of *Shawabti*-figures was a small wooden coffin, about thirty inches in length, fashioned like a coffin for a noble of the period. It contained a second coffin of gesso-gilt wood, ornamented after the fashion of a royal coffin, but neither of these two coffins bore royal emblems, although the formulas inscribed upon them give the names of Tutankhamen. The second coffin contained a third small plain wood coffin, and, beside it, a solid gold statuette of Amen-hetep III rolled up in a separate piece of mummy cloth. Within this third coffin was a fourth, also made of wood, man-shaped, but not more than five inches in length. This last coffin was wrapped in linen, tied at the neck with a band of minute beadwork, sealed at the ankles, and profusely annointed with unguents. It bore the titles and name of Queen Tyi, and, within it, care-fully folded in linen, was a plaited lock of her hair.

Such heirlooms as these—a lock of auburn hair of the Great Hereditary Princess, the Great Royal Wife, the Lady of the Two Lands, Tyi, and a statuette of her sovereign husband, Amenhetep III—are evidence of devotion. They were probably pieces of personal pro-perty that had been descending by due succession in the family. Tutankhamen, the ultimate heir, was the last of that ruling Amenhetep house; hence these heirlooms were buried with him. The gold statuette suspended on a chain was a trinket and was treated as such; the lock of hair was human, the remains of a royal personage, and therefore it received the prerogative of a royal burial.

But even more extraordinary were the contents of two miniature coffins that were placed, head to foot, in a wooden box beside the above-mentioned coffins. These were also fashioned in the manner used for a high personage. Each contained an inner gilt coffin of similar design. In one of them was a small mummy, preserved in accordance with burial custom of the Eighteenth Dynasty. It had a gesso-gilt mask (several sizes too large for it) covering its head. The linen wrap-pings enveloped a well-preserved mummy of a stillborn child. The other contained a slightly larger mummy of a child of premature birth, also wrapped in the pre-scribed fashion of the period.

There is little doubt that these pathetic remains were the offspring of Tutankhamen, and, probably, the issue of Ankhesenamen. Possibly, these *two* premature births were due merely to chance; the outcome of an abnormality of the young queen. However, it must not be forgotten that an accident to the expectant mother would have rendered the throne vacant for those eager to step in.

As I have mentioned, the coffins were placed side by side, head to feet, in a box. We noted with interest that the toes of the foot of the larger coffin had been hacked off because they prevented the lid of the box from closing properly, as had occurred in the case of the king's outer coffin. Another curious fact lies in the absence of a mask over the mummy of the larger child. In the cache discovered by Theodore M. Davis, where remnants from the burial ceremonies of Tutankhamen were found, there was a gesso-gilt mask of similar dimensions and character to that found here on the smaller child. Could it be that it was intended for this larger mummy, and was omitted because it was too small to fit over the head?

In the northwest corner of this chamber, leaning against the wall, was the king's bow case, the principal theme of ornament being idealized hunting scenes in which the king is the central figure. Towards the tapering ends of the case, which terminate in violet faience heads of cheetahs with gilded manes, are small symbolic scenes where the king, represented as a human-headed lion, tramples upon Egypt's alien foes. The central panels, of embossed gold, represent the king in his chariot, hunting with bow and arrow, accompanied by his hounds, depicted running beside or in front of his steeds, barking, or harassing the quarry. The triangular panels on either side represent various desert animals—stricken by the king's arrows.

This bow case evidently belonged to one of the king's hunting chariots that were found dismantled in this room, to which it was fastened by means of copper attachments expressly made for this purpose. It contained three neatly made composite bows.

With the dismembered parts of two hunting chariots found in this chamber, was a whip bearing an inscription : "The King's son, Captain of the Troops, Thoth-mes." Who was this royal prince who, to have been "Captain of the Troops," during the reign of Tutan-khamen could not have been very young? Was he a son of Thothmes IV or of Amenhetep III? That problem has yet to be solved. If he was a son of Thothmes IV, and was living at the time of Tutankhamen's burial, he must have reached the age of at least sixty; whereas if he was a son of Amenhetep III, he could not have been more than thirty-five at the time of Tutankha-men's death.

CHAPTER SEVENTEEN

THE ANNEXE

During the last days of November, 1927, we were able
to begin the final stage of our investigations, the clearing of the Annexe.

The doorway of the Annexe, only fifty-one inches
high and thirty-seven inches wide, had been blocked
with rough splinters of limestone and was plastered
over on the outside. The plaster, while still wet, had received numerous impressions of four different sepulchral seals of the king. Now only the upper part of the
blocking remained, the thieves having broken through
the lower portion. It was through this hole that we made
our first inspection of the room.

The room, comparatively small—fourteen feet long,
eight feet, six inches wide, and eight feet, five inches
high—gave no suggestion of any kind of finish, nor paid
any tribute to taste. It is roughly cut out of the bedrock,
and was intended for its purpose—a storeroom.

In contrast to the comparative order of the contents
of the Innermost Treasury, we found in this last chamber a jumble of every kind of funerary article, tumbled
any which way, almost defying description. Bedsteads,
chairs, stools, footstools, hassocks, game boards, baskets
of fruit, every kind of alabaster vessel and pottery wine
jar, boxes of funerary figures, toys, shields, bows and
arrows, and other missiles, all turned topsy-turvy.
Caskets thrown over, their contents spilled; in fact, it
would be difficult to exaggerate the confusion that
existed. It was an illustration of both drama and
tragedy. We felt that we could visualize the robbers'
hurried scramble for loot—gold and other metals being
their natural objectives; everything else they seem to
have treated in the most brutal fashion. There was

hardly an object that did not bear marks of depredation, and before us—upon one of the larger boxes—were the very foot-prints of the last intruder.

In the other chambers there had been a perfunctory attempt to restore order. The responsibility for this utter neglect would therefore seem to rest a good deal on the necropolis officials, who, in their task to put to rights the Antechamber, the Burial Chamber, and the Innermost Treasury after the robbery, had neglected this little room altogether.

Traces of the dilapidations of time were visible; the rock-cut walls and ceiling were discoloured by damp. Our electric lamps threw a mass of light on the room's crowded contents, bringing out many odd features in strong relief. Close to us, turned upside down, was a large chair like a folding stool, decorated in the taste of a distant age. Stretching across the room and resting precariously on their sides were bedsteads of a form still used today in the regions of the Upper Nile. Here a vase, and there a tiny figure gazed at one with forlorn expression.

There was something almost humorous, yet pathetic, in the situation of a small white chair possibly from the royal nursery, high-backed, animal-footed, turned upside-down among such plebeian society as oil and wine jars, and hampers of fruits, with which it was obliged to associate. Like its companion stool with gilded ornament between its seat and stretchers, it clung to the bedsteads of the royal household. Jammed down below the door-sill of the chamber, and crushed by heavy stone vessels, was another stool, also painted white, but in this case three-legged and with semi-circular seat. This somewhat ornate specimen has an open carved wood seat representing two lions bound head to tail. The rim is decorated with a spiral pattern. Like its companions just described, the space between the stretchers that brace the framework of the legs is filled in with open-work traditional throne ornament—the "Two Kingdoms"—Upper and Lower Egypt—bound together under the monarchy. In addition to its peculiar shape, it has a particular feature of its own which makes it in some ways unique. Most Egyptian chairs and stools have either the conventional bovine and feline or sometimes duck-headed legs, whereas the legs of this semicircular stool are of canine form.

Opposite the doorway, on the top of the material stacked against the west wall, was a rush-work garden-chair. The seat and back were covered, and the sides of the under-framework trimmed, with painted papyrus. The painted decoration on the back consisted of petals of the lotus-corolla, and on the seat the "Nine Bows," i.e. bound Asiatic and African prisoners in elaborate costume. The rush-work (mostly split papyrus stalks) and the papyrus covering, were too far decayed to allow of more than a few fragments being preserved.

Over and above the specimens just described there were many broken boxes. With the exception of one chest, they are all of somewhat rough make. Of these I will mention the examples that have a particular interest attached to them. One chest is of far more solid make than any box we have found in this tomb, and the few remains of its contents throw light upon the interests and amusements of a child of the Egyptian New Empire. The interior of the chest is fitted with complicated partitions, and with box-shaped drawers that are made to slide one above the other, and each provided with a sliding lid. These fittings had suffered from rough treatment; they had been wrenched open by impatient hands, evidently in search of what valuable material they may have contained. The chest was apparently for knick-knacks and playthings of Tutankhamen's youth, but, unfortunately, everything in it had been turned topsy-turvy; moreover, we found many of its trinkets strewn on the floor. A few of the things that we were able to recover were : a quantity of bracelets and anklets of ivory, wood, glass and leather; pocket game-boards of ivory; slings for hurling stones; gloves; a "lighter"; some leather archer's "bracers," to protect the left wrist from the blow of the bow-string; mechanical toys; some samples of minerals; and even pigments and paint-pots of the youthful painter. The exterior of this chest is decorated with the names and titles of the king, as well as with dedications to various gods. Its lid opens on heavy bronze hinges; the fastening of the knob upon the lid is so notched on the inside that when the lid was closed and the knob turned, it locked the lid to the box. This contrivance, I believe, is the earliest automatic fastening hitherto known. The chest itself, some $25\frac{1}{2}$ by 13 by $10\frac{1}{2}$ inches in size, stands on four square feet capped with bronze, and, pegged on the centre of its back frame, is a large wooden *ded*-amulet signifying "stability."

Scattered around were weapons of various kinds, baskets, pottery and alabaster jars, and gaming boards crushed and mingled with stones that had fallen from the hole that had been forced through the sealed doorway. In an opposite corner, poised high up, as if in a state of indecision, was a broken box bulging with delicate faience vessels, ready to collapse at any moment. In the midst of this miscellany a cabinet upon slender legs stood almost unscathed. Wedged between boxes and under objects of many shapes, were a boat of alabaster, a lion, and a figure of a bleating ibex. A fan, a sandal, a fragment of a robe, a glove keeping odd company with emblems of the living and of the dead. In fact the scene, seemed almost as if contrived with theatrical artifice to bewilder the beholder.

The method we finally adopted to remove those three-hundred-odd pieces of antiquity was somewhat prosaic. To begin with, sufficient floor space had to be made for our feet, and that had to be done as best we could, heads downward, bending over the door step, which was more than three feet above the floor level. Whilst carrying out this uncomfortable operation, we had to take every precaution lest a hasty movement should cause an avalanche of antiquities precariously piled up and beyond our reach. Often, to save a heavy object so situated that the slightest disturbance would cause it to fall, we were obliged to lean over and reach far out, supported by a rope-sling under our armpits, held by three or four men standing in the Antechamber. In that manner, by always removing one by one of the uppermost objects in reach, we gained entrance and gradually collected the treasures. Each object, or group of objects, had first to be photographed, numbered, and recorded, before it was moved.

I must confess that my first impression was that the positions of those objects were meaningless, and that there was little or nothing to be learned from such disorder. But as we proceeded in our investigations, it became evident that much data could be gleaned as to their original order and subsequent chaos. Careful examination of the facts disclosed one important point : two separate thefts of quite different nature had taken place in that little apartment. The first theft—for gold, silver, and bronze—was perpetrated by the famous tomb metal robbers, who ransacked the four chambers of the tomb for all such portable material. The second robbery was evidently by another class of thief, who sought only the costly oils and unguents contained in the numerous stone vessels. It also became clear that this Annexe was intended for a store room for housing oils, unguents, wine, and food, like the similar small chambers in other royal tombs of the Eighteenth Dynasty. But in this case an overflow of other material belonging to the burial equipment had been stacked on top of the room's proper contents.

The material that might be termed extraneous was probably put there, not so much for lack of space elsewhere, but probably owing to the absence of system when the equipment was being placed in the tomb. For example, below the Hathor-couch in the Antechamber there was a pile of uniform wooden cases containing a variety of meats. Those should have been stored in the Annexe. But owing to some oversight they seem to have been forgotten, and, the doorway of the Annexe having been closed, they had to be put in some convenient place in the Antechamber, which, in natural sequence, was the last room of the tomb to be closed. Also, part of the series of funerary boats and figures (*shawabtis*), placed in the Innermost Treasury were found in this Annexe.

From the facts gleaned we may reconstruct the sequence of events that took place : firstly, nearly forty pottery wine jars were placed on the floor at the northern end of the Annexe, next to these were added at least thirty-five heavy alabaster vessels containing oils and unguents; stacked beside them, some even on top, were 116 baskets of fruit; the remaining space was then used for furniture—boxes, stools, chairs, and bedsteads —that were piled on top of them. The doorway was then closed and sealed. This was carried out before any material was placed in the Antechamber, since nothing could have been passed into this Annexe, nor could the doorway have been closed, after the introduction of the materials belonging to the Antechamber.

When the metal robbers made their first incursion, they evidently crept under the Thueris couch in the Antechamber, forced their way through the sealed doorway of the Annexe, ransacked its entire contents for portable metal objects, and were, no doubt, responsible for a great deal of the disorder found in that chamber. Subsequently—it is impossible to say when— a second robbery took place. Its objective was the costly oils and unguents contained in the alabaster jars. This last robbery had been carefully thought out. The stone vessels being far too heavy and cumbersome to carry away, the thieves came provided with some more convenient receptacles, such as leather bags or water skins, to take away the spoil. There was not a stopper of a jar that had not been removed, not a jar that had not been emptied. The fingerprints of those thieves are visible today on the interior walls of some of the vessels that had contained sticky ointments. To get at those heavy stone vessels, the furniture piled on top of them was evidently turned over and thrown helter-skelter from side to side.

The knowledge of this second robbery throws light upon a problem that had puzzled us ever since the beginning of the discovery of the tomb. Why, throughout its funerary equipment, had quite insignificant stone vessels been tampered with? Why were some of them left empty lying on the floors of the chambers, and others taken out and discarded in the entrance passage? The greases or oils that they once contained had no doubt a far greater value in those days than we can imagine. It also explains why the tomb was twice reclosed, as traces on the sealed entrances and inner doorway of the passage signified. I believe also that the odd baskets and simple alabaster jars that were found scattered on the floor of the Antechamber came from the group in the Annexe. They are obviously of the same class and were probably taken out for convenience by the thieves. The same argument holds true of the solitary *Shawabti*-figure discovered leaning against the north wall of the Antechamber. It surely came from one of the broken *Shawabti*-boxes in the Annexe—for others like it were found there.

Tradition holds that in burial custom each article belonging to tomb equipment had its prescribed place in the tomb. However, no matter how true the governing conventions may be, seldom were they strictly carried out. Either the lack of forethought with regard to space, or the lack of system when placing the elaborate paraphernalia in the tomb chambers overcame tradition. We have never found any strict order, we have found only approximate order.

We have found evidence in this tomb of love and respect mingled with want of order and eventual dishonour. This tomb, though it did not wholly share the fate of its kindred, though mightier, mausoleums, was nevertheless robbed—twice robbed—in Pharaornic times. I think that both robberies took place within a few years of the burial. The transfer of Akhenaten's mummy from its original tomb at Tell el-Amarna to its rock-cut cell at Thebes, apparently within the reign of Tutankhamen, and the renewal of the burial of Thothmes IV, in the eighth year of the reign of Horemheb, after his tomb had been robbed of its treasures, throw considerable light upon the state of affairs in the royal necropolis at that age. The religious confusion of the state at that time; the collapse of the Eighteenth Dynasty; the retention of the throne by the Grand Chamberlain (and probably Regent), Ay, who was eventually supplanted by General Horemheb, were incidents which we may assume helped towards the general unrest in which such forms of pillage flourished. It must have been a considerable time before even the conquering Horemheb was able to restore order out of the confusion that existed at that period, establish his kingdom and enforce the law of his state. In any case, the evidence afforded by those two burials and by this tomb prove how the royal tombs suffered even within their own Dynasty. The wonder is that Tutankhamen's tomb, this royal burial with all its riches, escaped the eventual fate of the twenty-seven others in the Valley.

CHAPTER EIGHTEEN

TUTANKHAMEN

Whenever an archaeological discovery lays bare traces of a remote age, and the vanished human lives it fostered, we turn at once instinctively to the facts revealed to us with which we are most in sympathy.

This is, to a certain extent, true of the discovery of the tomb of Tutankhamen.

If tradition and priestly practice governed ancient Egyptian burial ceremonial, so their ritual left room for a more private aspect. The impression of a personal sorrow is perhaps more distinctly conveyed to us from what we learn from the tomb of Tutankhamen than by most other discoveries. The tiny wreath on the stately coffin, the beautiful alabaster wishing-cup with its touching inscription, the treasured reed with its suggestive memories—cut by the young king himself by the lake-side.

The sense of premature loss faintly haunts the tomb. The royal youth, obviously full of life and capable of enjoying it, had started, in very early manhood—on his last journey into the gloom of that tremendous Underworld. How could grief be best expressed? In his tomb we are conscious of this effort, and the emotion gently and gracefully exhibited is the expression of that human regret which joins our sympathies to a sorrow more than three thousand years old.

Politically we gather that the king's brief reign and life must have been a singularly uneasy one. It may be that he was the tool of obscure political forces working behind the throne. This, at least from the information that we have found, is a reasonable conjecture. But however much Tutankhamen may have been the tool of political religious movements, whatever political influence the youthful king may have possessed, or whatever his own religious feelings, if any, may have been—and this must remain uncertain—we do gather knowledge of to his tastes and inclinations from the innumerable scenes on the furniture of his tomb. It is in these that we find the most vivid suggestions of Tutankhamen's affectionate domestic relations with the young queen, and that evidence of his love of sport, of the royal and youthful passion for the chase, which makes him so human to our sympathies after the lapse of so many dark centuries.

What could be more charming than the tableau upon the throne, so touchingly represented? Ankhesenamen, the charming girlish wife, is seen adding a touch of perfume to the young king's collar, or putting the last touches to his toilet before he enters into some great function in the palace. Nor must we forget that little wreath of flowers, still retaining their tinge of colour, that farewell offering placed upon the brow of the young king's effigy as he lay within his quartzite sarcophagus.

Other incidents represented suggest even a touch of humour. Among episodes of the daily private life of the king and queen on a small golden *naos*, we find Tutankhamen accompanied by his lion-cub, shooting wild-duck with bow and arrow, whilst, at his feet, squats the girlish queen. With one hand she is handing him an arrow, while with the other she points out a fat duck. On the same *naos* the young wife is represented offering him sacred libations, flowers and collarettes, or tying a pendant around his neck. Here we have the young couple in various simple and engaging attitudes. The queen accompanies the king on another fowling expedition in a reed canoe. She is seen affectionately supporting his arm as though he was wearied by state affairs, and then again—and there is a suggestion of playfulness in these little glimpses of their private life—we find him pouring sweet perfume on her hand as they are resting in their cabinet. These are charming scenes and full of the kindliness which it pleases us to consider modern.

Upon a golden fan is a beautifully embossed and chased picture of Tutankhamen, hunting ostriches for the plumes for that very flabellum. On its reverse side he is seen returning home triumphant, his attendants carrying his quarry—two dead ostriches—and the coveted feathers under his arm.

Scenes of the young sportsman's activities constantly confront us. Upon trappings of the chariot-harness he is shown practising archery. We gather, too, that, like some of our earlier kings, he was a lover of the bow. And, as proof of his proficiency in archery, there was treasured in his tomb, among boomerangs and similar missiles of the chase, a magnificent bow-of-honour, covered with sheet-gold, decorated with fine filigree gold-work, and richly adorned with semi-precious stones and coloured glass. Lying nearest to him, under the golden shrines that shielded his sarcophagus, were other bows and arrows. The sheath of a handsome gold dagger, found girded to his waist within the wrappings of his mummy, has also wild animals embossed upon it. Even his cosmetic jar bears evidence of his pastime. On it are portrayed bulls, lions, hounds, gazelles and hare —the huntsman's favourite game. His slughi hounds are especially included in scenes suggesting fondness of field sport and of an open-air life. We have striking evidence of this in a delightful and vigorous sketch found while nearing the entrance of his tomb, and possibly drawn by one of the artisans employed in making the sepulchre : it is on a flake of limestone and represents the young king, aided by his slughi hounds, slaying a lion with a spear.

Evidences of the kindlier affections are traits we scarcely expect to find among a Pharaoh's relics, and we are surprised, as well as touched, by the expression of simpler human feelings charmingly portrayed on Tutankhamen's funerary furniture. From them we gather that he was a gallant and amiable youth, loving horse and hound, sport and military display. But there is another side to the picture. The traditional ornament, worked in gold on the chariots, the beautiful carving of African and Asiatic prisoners bound to the king's walking-sticks, and on his furniture all suggest the formidable Pharaoh, bent, metaphorically at least, on "making his enemy his footstool", and typify the braggart spirit associated with the character of Egypt's ancient rulers, although as we have it here, it is less overwhelmingly expressed than in other tombs.

The silver trumpets dedicated to the legions or units of the Egyptian army, found in the Antechamber and Burial Chamber, appeal to the imagination. The military experience of Tutankhamen must have been small indeed, but we may nevertheless imagine him surrounded by his generals, state officials and courtiers, taking the salute whilst the massed legions in military pageant went by.

His mummy, like his statues, shows him to have been a slim youth with large head, presenting structural resemblance to the dreamer Ankhenaten, who in all probability was not only his father-in-law but also his father.

Thus step by step, the excavator's spade is revealing to us the world of the past, and the more our knowledge extends, the greater grows our wonder—possibly our regret—that human nature should have so little changed during the few thousand years of which we have some historical knowledge. Especially our gaze is fixed on ancient Egypt which has given us such vivid glimpses of a wonderful past. On painted casket, decorated chair, on shrine, tomb chapel or temple wall, her ancient life passes in strange and moving pageant. In many points our sympathies meet, but it is chiefly by her art that we are brought nearest to her feeling, and that we recognize in the royal sportsman, the dog-lover, the young husband and the slender wife, creatures in human taste, emotion and affection, very like ourselves. And so we learn not to overvalue the present, and our modern perspective becomes less complacent and more philosophical. There are atavisms of which we are barely conscious, and it may be these that awaken in us sympathy for the youthful Tutankhamen, for his queen, and all the life suggested by his funerary furniture. It may be these instincts which make us yearn to unravel the mystery of those dim political intrigues by which we suspect he was beset, even whilst following his slughi hounds across marsh and desert, or shooting duck among the reeds with his smiling queen. The mystery of his life still eludes us—the shadows move but the dark is never quite uplifted.

APPENDIX ONE

REPORT ON THE EXAMINATION OF TUTANKHAMEN'S MUMMY

by Douglas E. Derry, MB, Ch.B

The examination of the mummy of King Tutankhamen was begun on 11 November 1925, body and limbs.

Some of the linen use in the wrapping of the king was of the nature of the finest cambric, notably that first encountered when the examination was commenced and again immediately next to the body itself. The intermediate bandages were of coarser make, and at one stage folded sheets of linen were placed along the front of the body as far as the knees and retained in place by transverse bandages. The practice of using immense quantities of linen in the form of folded sheets appears to have been common in the Twelfth Dynasty, one such sheet, removed by myself from the mummy of a noble, measured 64 feet in length by 5 feet in width, this being folded to produce a covering eight layers thick. In his account of the removal of the bandages from the mummy styled Amenhetep III (*loc. cit. supra*) Professor Elliot Smith notes the presence of several folded sheets, as well as "a number of rolls of bandage . . . in front of the body, apparently left there inadvertently." These latter may well have been employed originally to fill up the spaces and inequalities existing between the limbs and body, a practice frequently seen in mummies of all periods, and with the same object as in the case where they were used in connection with the funerary ornaments placed on the body. Over the thorax the bandages were made to pass alternately in crossed and transverse layers, the crossed bandages being carried over one shoulder then round the body returning over the opposite shoulder.

In the crutch the crossed arrangements of the bandages was easily visible, though the method used to produce this could not be followed out, both on account of the fragility of the wrappings and the fact that the body could not be moved at this stage from the coffin.

All the limbs were separately wrapped before being enclosed by the bandages which enveloped the body as a whole. The upper limbs were so placed that the king lay with his forearms across his body, the right forearm resting on the upper part of the abdomen with the hand on the crest of the left hip bone. The left forearm lay higher up over the lower ribs, with the hand lying on right upper-arm. Both forearms were loaded with bracelets from the bend of the elbow to the wrist. All fingers and toes were bandaged individually and gold sheaths were then adjusted over each before the bandage covering in the whole hand or foot was applied. In the case of the feet gold sandals were put on at the same time as the toe-sheaths and after the first few layers of bandage had been applied, in order to allow the bar of the sandal to be adjusted between the great and second toes—the whole being then enclosed in a bandage.

When first exposed, the upper part of the bandaged head was seen to be surrounded by a double fillet which overlay a bandage encircling the head. This fillet, which somewhat resembled a Bedouin head-rope, but of a much smaller diameter, was composed of some sort of vegetable fibre around which twine had been tightly wound. The circular bandage in its turn held in place a sheet which passed over the head and face. Beneath this sheet the bandages passed alternately across the head and transversely round the head and face. When the face was finally exposed some resinous material was found plugging the nostrils, and a layer had been placed over the eyes and between the lips.

General appearance of head : The head appears to be clean-shaved and the skin of the scalp is covered by a whitish substance probably of the nature of fatty acid. Two abrasions on the skin covering the upper part of the occipital bone, had probably been caused by the pressure of the diadem which was enclosed by the tightly-wound head bandages. The plugs filling the nostrils and the material laid over the eyes were found by Mr. Lucas to consist of some woven fabric, impregnated with resin. Mr. Lucas also examined some whitish spots on the skin over the upper part of the back and shoulders, and these proved to be composed of "common salt with a small admixture of sodium sulphate" in all probability derived from the natron used in the embalming process. The eyes are partly open and had not been interfered with in any way. The eyelashes are very long. The cartilaginous portion of the nose had become partially flattened by the pressure of the bandages. The upper lip is slightly elevated revealing the large central incisor teeth. The ears are small and well made. The lobes of the ears are perforated by a circular hole measuring 7·5 mm. in diameter.

The skin of the face is of greyish colour and is very cracked and brittle. On the left cheek, just in front of the lobe of the ear, is a rounded depression, the skin filling it, resembling a scab. Round the circumference of the depression, which has slightly raised edges, the skin is discoloured. It is not possible to say what the nature of this lesion may have been.

The head when fully uncovered was seen to be very broad and flat topped (platycephalic) with markedly projecting occipital region. Even allowing for the shrinkage both of the scalp and the posterior muscles of the neck, this prominence is still remarkable. There is pronounced bulging of the left side of the occiput and the post-bregmatic region is depressed. The general shape of the head, which is of a very uncommon type, is so like that of his father-in-law, Akhenaten, that it is more than probable there was a close relationship in blood between these two kings. Such a statement made in regard to the normal type of Egyptian skull might justly be considered to have little weight, but the reality of the comparison is accentuated when it is recalled that the remarkable shape of the skull of King Akhenaten led Professor Elliot Smith who first examined it in 1907, to the conclusion that the heretic king had suffered from a condition of hydrocephalus. Subsequent examination has not confirmed his theory, chiefly because the flattening of the cranium in Ahkenaten contrasts markedly with the shape of the head in known cases of hydrocephalus. In these the pressure of fluid in the brain acting upon the yielding walls of the cranium naturally produces a globular shape, particularly in the frontal region, which is quite the reverse of the condition observed in the skull of Akhenaten.

When, therefore, we find that Tutankhamen exhibits an almost exact reproduction of his father-in-law's head it not only disposes finally the theory of hydrocephalus, but makes the argument in favour of a very close relationship extremely convincing. This argument receives still greater weight when we compare the measurements of the two skulls. A breadth of 154 mm. in Akhenaten is, as pointed out by Professor Elliot Smith, "quite an exceptional breadth for an Egyptian skull" yet in his son-in-law we have a breadth of 156·5 mm. When allowance is made for the thickness of the scalp, over which, in the case of Tutankhamen, all measurements were necessarily made, and which by a special instrument was found to be not more than 0·5 mm. in thickness, the breadth of the actual skull is 155·5 mm. exceeding therefore that of his father-in-law, which as we have seen is "quite exceptional." Corresponding measurements in the two skulls, so far as these may be justly compared under the different conditions of examination, show a remarkable similarity, and make the probability of blood relationship almost a certainty.

The effigy of Tutankhamen on the gold mask exhibits him as a gentle and refined-looking young man. Those who were privileged to see the actual face when finally exposed can bear testimony to the ability and accuracy of the Eighteenth Dynasty artist who has so faithfully represented the features, and left for all time, in imperishable metal, a beautiful portrait of the young king.

The skull cavity was empty except for some resinous material which had been introduced through the nose in the manner employed by the embalmers of the period, after they had extracted the brain by the same route.

The right upper and lower wisdom teeth had just erupted the gum and reached to about half the height of the second molar. Those on the left side were not so easily seen but appeared to be in the same stage of eruption.

General appearance of body and limbs : The cracked and brittle state of the skin of the head and face, already referred to, was even more marked in the body and limbs. The abdominal wall exhibited a marked bulging on the right side. This was found to be due to the forcing of the packing material across the abdominal cavity from the left side where the embalming incision is situated. This opening, which had a ragged appearance, is roughly 86 mm. in length and is placed parallel to a line drawn from the umbilicus to the anterior superior iliac spine and an inch above this line. This was only exposed after the removal of a carbonized mass of what was apparently resin, and the length of the incision may thereafter have been greater than is now apparent, as the hardness of the adherent mass made it difficult to define the limits of the wound. The lips of the wound are inverted owing to the forcible packing of the abdomen with a mass of linen and resin, now of rock-like hardness. The plate of gold or wax so frequently found covering the embalming wound was not present, but an oval plate of gold was found on the left side during the removal of the wrappings included amongst the layers of bandages and in the neighbourhood of the opening in the abdominal wall. The incision is situated somewhat differently from that described by Professor Elliot Smith in the royal mummies he examined; in these it was usually placed more vertically and in the left flank, extending from near the lower ribs to the anterior superior iliac spine. At a later period the incision was more often made in the lower part of the abdominal wall, parallel with the line of the groin, but always on the left side, but there were occasional reversions to the older site and it seems questionable whether the position had any significance. There was no pubic hair visible, nor was it possible to say whether circumcision had been performed, but the phallus had been drawn forward, wrapped independently, and then retained in the ithyphallic position by the perineal bandages.

The skin of the legs, like that of the rest of the body, was of a greyish-white colour, very brittle and exhibiting numerous cracks. Examination of a piece of this showed that it consisted not only of the skin but of all the soft parts down to the bone, which was thus laid bare when such a piece came away, the whole thickness of skin and tissues in this situation being not more than two or three millimetres. The fractured edges resembled glue. There is little doubt that this was produced by the combustion referred to. The left patella and skin covering it could be lifted off and the lower end of the femur was thus exposed, showing the epiphysis which was found to be separate from the shaft and freely moveable. The term epiphysis is applied to that part of a bone which ossifies separately and which eventually becomes fused to the main bone. In the limb bones the epiphyses form the chief part of the upper and lower ends. During early life they are attached to the main bone by cartilage which finally becomes completely converted into bone and growth then ceases. The average date of union of all the epiphyses is known, hence the approximate age can be estimated in any case where union is still incomplete.

The limbs appeared very shrunken and attenuated, but even when due allowance is made for the extreme shrinking of the tissues, and the appearance of emaciation which this produces, it is still evident that Tutankhamen must have been of slight build and perhaps not fully grown at the time of his death.

Direct measurements made him about 5 feet $4\frac{1}{4}$ inches in height, but this is almost certainly less than his stature during life, owing to the shrinkage referred to. An estimate of living height from the measurements yielded by the principal limb bones calculated according to the formulae devised by Professor Karl Pearson gives a stature of 1·676 metres (5 feet 6 inches), which is probably very near the actual truth. With the assistance of Mr. R. Engelbach, the writer measured the two wooden statues of the young king, now in the Museum of Antiquities, which stood on either side of the sealed door leading to the Burial Chamber, and which represent him as he appeared in life. Measurements were made from the root of the nose to the sole of the foot, the nasion being the only anatomical point on the heads of the statues which could be located with any degree of accuracy, as the actual height of the head is obscured in the statues by the head-dress. In the two statues this measurement gave 1·592 metres and 1·602 metres respectively, as the height from sole of foot to root of nose. It was then necessary to add to this the calculated height from this point to the top of the head. This was estimated by measurements from the actual photographs of the king, as well as from a series of observations on Egyptian skulls, to amount to between 8 and 9 cm., which, added to the height of the statues already given, yields a result within a few millimetres of the calculated stature from the bones.

The evidence for the age of the king at the time of his death was obtained from the extent of union or otherwise of the epiphyses. As already mentioned, the cracked condition of the skin and tissues overlying the femur permitted a clear view of the lower ununited portion. This part unites with the shaft about the age of twenty. At the upper end of the thigh bone the prominence known as the great trochanter was almost entirely soldered to the main bone, but on its inner side a definite gap showing the smooth cartilaginous surface where union was still incomplete, could be well seen. This epiphysis joins about the eighteenth year. The head of the femur was fixed to the neck of the bone, but the line of union was clearly visible all round the articular margin. The epiphysis also unites about the eighteenth or nineteenth year. The upper end of the tibia was also ununited, but the lower end appeared to be quite fused. As this latter portion of the tibia is generally found to fuse with the shaft about the age of eighteen, Tutankhamen, from the evidence of his lower limbs, would appear to have been over eighteen but below twenty years of age at the date of his death.

But we are not limited to these bones for evidence of age. It was possible to examine the upper limbs. Here the heads of the humeri, or upper-arm bones, which join about twenty, are still not united, but the lower ends are completely joined to the shaft. In modern Egyptians of seventeen years of age the lower end is seen to be quite fused to the shaft as well as the epiphysis capping the internal condyle, when examined by X-rays, so that if what obtains in Egypt today can be applied to the young king, Tutankhamen was evidently over seventeen when he died.

The lower ends of the radius and ulna in modern Egyptians show little or no union in most cases until the age of eighteen, after which date they fuse fairly rapidly. The union begins on the inner side of the ulna and proceeds laterally, gradually involving the radius. In Tutankhamen fusion appeared to have begun in the ulna, but the distal end of the radius is entirely free, no bony union whatever having commenced between the shaft and its epiphysis. From the state of the epiphyses above described it would appear that the king was about eighteen years of age at the time of his death. None of the epiphyses which should unite about the twentieth year shows any sign of union. There is evidence that in Egypt the epiphyses tend on the average to unite somewhat earlier than is the rule in Europe.

Mention has already been made of the epiphysis of the internal condyle of the humerus which in Egypt is joined completely to the shaft by about seventeen years of age, and of those of the lower end of the radius and ulan which begin to unite at about eighteen. The absence of any ossification here might be taken as evidence that Tutankhamen was less than eighteen at death, but against this we have the complete union of the lower end of the tibia, usually about eighteen, as well as the condition of affairs at the upper end of the femur where the great trochanter, which also joins about eighteen years of age, is, with the exception of a very small portion, fused to the main bone and the head of the same bone, although the line of union is clearly visible all round, is nevertheless joined to the neck.

There is thus little room for doubt as to the approximate age of the king, but it should be borne in mind that the dates given represent the average and that it is permissible to add or deduct about a year, so that Tutankhamen might be any age between seventeen and nineteen, but with the balance of evidence strongly in favour of the middle date, viz. eighteen.

The following table illustrates the similarity between

the measurements made on the skull of Akhenaten and those from the head of Tutankhamen.

	Akhenaten	Tutankhamen
Length of skull	190·0	187·0
Breadth of skull	154·0	155·5
Height of skull	134·0	132·5
Forehead breadth	98·0	99·0
Height of face : upper	69·5	73·5
Height of face : total	121·0	122·0
Breadth of jaw	99·5	99·0
Circumference of head	542·0	547·0
Height calculated from limb bones	1·66 metres (5ft. 5¼in.)	1·68 metres (5ft. 6 in.)

Although the examination of the young king afforded no clue to the cause of his early death, the investigation has added something at least to the few facts already known of the history of the period. The age of Tutankhamen at the time of his decease, and the likelihood that he was a blood relation of Akhenaten, are important evidence in the reconstruction of the events of the time, and will play their part when the history of that time comes to be written.

THE PHARAOHS

Egyptian chronology is still based on that of Manetho who wrote in the third century BC, and much of the dating is still disputed by modern scholars. The following table is taken from Cyril Aldred's study of AKHENATEN (Thames & Hudson, 1968).

ARCHAIC PERIOD Dynasties I–II *c.* 3100–2686 BC	Amenophis I 1534–1504 BC
	Tuthmosis I 1514–1502 BC
	Tuthmosis II 1504–1489 BC
OLD KINGDOM Dynasties III–VI *c.* 2686–2181 BC	Tuthmosis III 1490–1436 BC
	Hatshepsut 1489–1469 BC
	Amenophis II 1444–1412 BC
	Tuthmosis IV 1414–1405 BC
FIRST INTERMEDIATE PERIOD Dynasties VII–X *c.* 2181–2040 BC	Amenophis III 1405–1367 BC
	Amenophis IV } Akhenaten } 1378–1362 BC
MIDDLE KINGDOM Dynasties XI–XIII *c.* 2060–1674 BC	Smekh-ka-Re 1366–1363 BC
	Tutankhamen 1362–1353 BC
	Ay 1353–1349 BC
SECOND INTERMEDIATE PERIOD Dynasties XIV–XVII *c.* 1674–1559 BC	Har-em-hab 1349–1319 BC
	DYNASTY XIX
	Rameses I 1320–1318 BC
NEW KINGDOM Dynasties XVIII–XX *c.* 1559–1085 BC	Sethos I 1318–1304 BC
	Rameses II 1304–1237 BC
	and six other rulers to 1200 BC
DYNASTY XVIII	**DYNASTY XX**
Amosis 1559–1531 BC	1200–1085 BC